T0323941

Rock around the Clock

Examining one of the earliest films made specifically for young audiences in US cinema, *Rock around the Clock* (1956), this book explores the exploitation production company that made the film and the ways it represented young people, especially in terms of their association with rock 'n' roll music and culture.

Providing new avenues of approaching the film, the book looks at how *Rock around the Clock* has attracted significant scholarly attention, despite its origins as a low-budget production made by master exploitation filmmaker Sam Katzman. It challenges accounts that see the film's young people as juvenile delinquents, using instead the label 'cultural rebels' as a signifier of youth's ability to resurrect a moribund music industry and rejuvenate a stale youth culture. This book also questions the nature of the label 'exploitation' as applied to the film by examining Columbia Pictures' role as a resource provider for Katzman's film, comparing *Rock around the Clock* to contemporaneous films with a youth focus that were produced in different industrial contexts and investigating its relationship to adaptation by asking whether the film is an example of a 'postliterary' adaptation.

Rich on archival research and industrial and textual analysis, *Rock around the Clock* will interest both film studies and youth cultures scholars.

Yannis Tzioumakis is Reader in Film and Media Industries at the University of Liverpool. He is the author of five books and co-editor of seven collections. His next book is a monograph under the title *When Hollywood Came to Greece, 1957–1967*, after which he will be co-authoring a volume on the 100-year history of Paramount. Yannis also co-edits the Routledge Hollywood Centenary and the Cinema and Youth Cultures book series.

Siân Lincoln is an independent scholar who has published widely on aspects of youth cultures. Her monograph *Youth Culture and Private Space* was published in 2012 and her co-authored book with Brady Robards *Growing up on Facebook* was published in 2020. She is co-editor of two book series: Cinema and Youth Cultures and the Palgrave Studies in the History of Subcultures & Popular Music. Siân is on the management group of the Interdisciplinary Network for the Study of Music, Subcultures and Social Change.

Cinema and Youth Cultures

Cinema and Youth Cultures engages with well-known youth films from American cinema as well as the cinemas of other countries. Using a variety of methodological and critical approaches the series volumes provide informed accounts of how young people have been represented in film, while also exploring the ways in which young people engage with films made for and about them. In doing this, the Cinema and Youth Cultures series contributes to important and long-standing debates about youth cultures, how these are mobilized and articulated in influential film texts and the impact that these texts have had on popular culture at large.

Series Editors: Siân Lincoln and Yannis Tzioumakis

Mustang
Translating Willful Youth
Elif Akçalı, Cüneyt Çakırlar, Özlem Güçlü

Mary Poppins
Radical Elevation in the 1960s
Leslie H. Abramson

The Outsiders
Adolescent Tenderness and Staying Gold
Ann M. Ciasullo

American Graffiti
George Lucas, the New Hollywood and the Baby Boom Generation
Peter Krämer

Before Sunrise
Young Love on the Move
María del Mar Azcona and Celestino Deleyto

Rock around the Clock
Exploitation, Rock 'n' Roll and the Origins of Youth Culture
Yannis Tzioumakis and Siân Lincoln

For more information about this series, please visit: https://www.routledge.com/Cinema-and-Youth-Cultures/book-series/CYC

Rock around the Clock
Exploitation, Rock 'n' Roll and the Origins of Youth Culture

Yannis Tzioumakis and Siân Lincoln

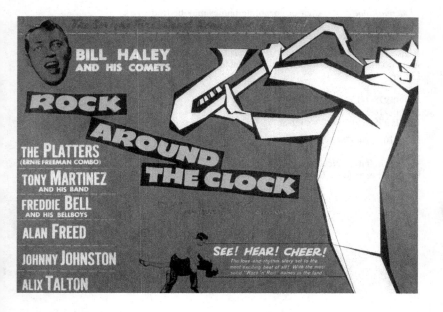

Poster for *Rock Around The Clock*, 1956. Image courtesy of Moviestore/ Shutterstock

 Routledge
Taylor & Francis Group

LONDON AND NEW YORK

First published 2024
by Routledge
4 Park Square, Milton Park, Abingdon, Oxon OX14 4RN

and by Routledge
605 Third Avenue, New York, NY 10158

*Routledge is an imprint of the Taylor & Francis Group, an informa
business*

© 2024 Yannis Tzioumakis and Siân Lincoln

The right of Yannis Tzioumakis and Siân Lincoln to be identified as
authors of this work has been asserted in accordance with sections
77 and 78 of the Copyright, Designs and Patents Act 1988.

All rights reserved. No part of this book may be reprinted or
reproduced or utilised in any form or by any electronic, mechanical,
or other means, now known or hereafter invented, including
photocopying and recording, or in any information storage or
retrieval system, without permission in writing from the publishers.

Trademark notice: Product or corporate names may be trademarks
or registered trademarks, and are used only for identification and
explanation without intent to infringe.

British Library Cataloguing-in-Publication Data
A catalogue record for this book is available from the British
Library

ISBN: 978-1-138-68277-1 (hbk)
ISBN: 978-1-032-58795-0 (pbk)
ISBN: 978-1-315-54490-8 (ebk)

DOI: 10.4324/9781315544908

Typeset in Times New Roman
by Taylor & Francis Books

For Roman

Contents

Figures

Series Editors' Introduction

Despite the high visibility of youth films in the global media marketplace (especially since the 1980s, when Conglomerate Hollywood realised that such films were not only strong box-office performers but also the starting point for ancillary sales in other media markets as well as for franchise building), academic studies that focused specifically on such films were slow to materialise. Arguably the most important factor behind academia's reluctance to engage with youth films was a (then) widespread perception within the film and media studies communities that such films held little cultural value and significance, and therefore were not worthy of serious scholarly research and examination. Just like the young subjects they represented, whose interests and cultural practices have been routinely deemed transitional and transitory, so were the films that represented them perceived as fleeting and easily digestible, destined to be forgotten quickly, as soon as the next youth film arrived in cinema screens a week later.

Under these circumstances, and despite a small number of pioneering studies in the 1980s and early 1990s, the field of 'youth film studies' did not really start blossoming and attracting significant scholarly attention until the 2000s and in combination with similar developments in cognate areas such as 'girl studies'. However, because of the paucity of material in the previous decades, the majority of these new studies in the 2000s focused primarily on charting the field and therefore steered clear of long, in-depth examinations of youth films or was exemplified by edited collections that chose particular films to highlight certain issues to the detriment of others. In other words, despite providing often wonderfully rich accounts of youth cultures as these have been captured by key films, these studies could not have possibly dedicate sufficient space to engage with more than just a few key aspects of youth films.

In more recent (post-2010) years, a number of academic studies started delimiting their focus and therefore providing more space for in-depth examinations of key types of youth films, such as slasher films and biker films or examining youth films in particular historical periods. From that point on, it was a matter of time for the first publications that focused exclusively on key youth films from a number of perspectives to appear (*Mamma Mia! The Movie, Twilight* and *Dirty Dancing* were among the first films to receive this treatment). Conceived primarily as edited collections, these studies provided a multifaceted analysis of these films, focusing on such issues as the politics of representing youth, the stylistic and narrative choices that characterise these films and the extent to which they are representative of a youth cinema, the ways these films address their audiences, the ways youth audiences engage with these films, the films' industrial location and other relevant issues.

It is within this increasingly maturing and expanding academic environment that the **Cinema and Youth Cultures** volumes arrive, aiming to consolidate existing knowledge, provide new perspectives, apply innovative methodological approaches, offer sustained and in-depth analyses of key films, and therefore become the 'go to' resource for students and scholars interested in theoretically informed, authoritative accounts of youth cultures in film. As editors, we have tried to be as inclusive as possible in our selection of key examples of youth films by commissioning volumes on films that span the history of cinema, including the silent film era; that portray contemporary youth cultures as well as ones associated with particular historical periods; that represent examples of mainstream and independent cinema; that originate in American cinema and the cinemas of other nations; that attracted significant critical attention and commercial success during their initial release and that were 'rediscovered' after an unpromising initial critical reception. Together these volumes are going to advance youth film studies while also being able to offer extremely detailed examinations of films that are now considered significant contributions to cinema and our cultural life more broadly.

We hope readers will enjoy the series.

Siân Lincoln and Yannis Tzioumakis
Cinema and Youth Cultures series editors

Acknowledgements

In 2012 we worked together for the first time, editing a volume on the land-mark 1987 film *Dirty Dancing*. Siân brought to that project her expertise in youth cultures; Yannis came to it from a film studies perspective. Our combined research expertise attracted to that volume a host of scholars from different fields and disciplines, all keen to examine the film from different angles and discuss its impact on popular culture.

That book prompted us to collaborate again by developing and co-editing the Cinema and Youth Cultures book series, and now co-authoring a volume for the series on the little-known but extremely influential film *Rock around the Clock* (1956), arguably the 'first rock 'n' roll film' in US cinema. We have both taught the film as part of 'Youth Cultures' and 'Hollywood Cinema' survey courses, respectively, and have always enjoyed seeing our students engage with questions of youth representation, whether these related to debates around subcultures and/or exploitation filmmaking.

Although these two 'frames' guided our own approach to researching the volume, our work put us into contact with a host of other issues, from rock 'n' roll's links to swing music to the organisation of the American film industry in the 1950s, to who has the power to tell the story of youth and how. In the process, we read wonderful work by other scholars, while our archival research brought us face to face with incredibly interesting material that sometimes questioned existing accounts and helped us reconsider aspects of our cultural history.

We would like to thank Natalie Foster for giving the Cinema and Youth Cultures series a home at Routledge and for greenlighting a volume on *Rock around the Clock*, even though it was not the most obvious title for the series. We would also like to thank Kelly O'Brien, who's been amazing in overseeing the administrative aspects of its publication.

Siân wants to thank Yannis for getting me into the film in the first place! Yannis suggested I teach it as part of my Youth Cultures module when I was still a university lecturer and I have loved the film ever since. I would like to give a special mention to my dearest friend Paula Casson, who has tolerated my attempts at rock 'n' roll dancing in many a kitchen disco over the years! I am very fortunate to have a great friendship group of strong, inspiring women who support me in whatever I do and never fail to be interested and interesting. They are: Alice Ferrebe, Shelley Lockett, Amy Causley, Annalies McIver, Athena Tanabasi, Alex Cookson, Laura Hardman, Debbie Redcliffe, Christine Feldman-Barrett, Fiona O'Mahony and Carys Damon. Thank you!

Yannis wants to thank the University of Liverpool School of the Arts for generously supporting visits to the Margaret Herrick Library for research and for helping with the purchase of some of the images for the volume; Peter Krämer and Peter Stanfield for reading the manuscript and offering valuable advice; Pamela Robertson Wojcik for providing advice with particular sources; Gary Needham for managing to locate obscure rock 'n' roll and swing films to watch as context; Julia Hallam for sharing stories about the cinemas in Liverpool where the film was shown; Dave Maher for his insights on the film's reception by Liverpool's Merseybeat community; and Sheldon Hall for inviting me to Sheffield Hallam University in June 2022 to present this work, following a screening of *Rock around the Clock* in a glorious 35mm copy. I would also like to thank my parents Panayiotis (who saw *Rock around the Clock* as a teenager in Greece in the late 1950s) and Christina, my brother Leonidas, as well as my good friends Rigas Goulimaris, Harris Tlas and Panayiotis Koutakis.

Finally, we would both like to extend a special thank you to Colin Fallows, a close friend, big supporter of our work and the person who inspired us to develop the Cinema and Youth Cultures series.

This book is dedicated to our son, Roman. In the process of doing all this work, Roman sat with us and watched countless films from a very young age, developing a real passion for both film and music, and helping make this project a true family experience! We can't quite put him down as a co-author but we are incredibly happy to dedicate this book to him!

Introduction
From Exploitation to Legitimacy

When *Rock around the Clock* (Sears, 1956) was released in North American theatres on 21 March 1956 few could have predicted its spectacular commercial success, its significance as a trendsetting picture that would initiate a cycle of films about rock 'n' roll and its impact on the emerging film genre of the teen film. Even fewer would have expected that the film would receive largely positive reviews by critics, despite reports that its music enticed some young people to behave in an unruly fashion while watching the film in theatres around the world. It is highly doubtful, however, that anyone would have expected that the film would be slowly but surely canonised as a culturally significant work and that it would attract a substantial volume of academic writing (and now a book) dedicated to it.

The reason behind these low expectations is that *Rock around the Clock* originated as a production in the so-called exploitation film sector of the US film industry, even though it reached the theatres under the veneer of a major Hollywood studio-distributor, Columbia Pictures. Although the term 'exploitation' as pertains to American cinema has had a number of meanings throughout its history, by the mid-1950s, when *RATC* was released, it was understood in a very particular context. Exploitation had become associated with low-budget films that were conceived around an easily marketable premise that would then be exploited by distributors without the help of elements that normally bring to a film commercial value (the presence of stars, international location shooting, colour photography, spectacle, a narrative premise based on a presold property such as a play or a novel, etc.) but which come at a cost that only a relatively small number of companies could afford.

Taking this initial definition of exploitation as a starting point, one could argue that *Rock around the Clock* was the epitome of exploitation film. Its narrative is rather schematic and revolves around the

DOI: 10.4324/9781315544908-1

efforts of a band manager, Steve Hollis (Johnny Johnston), to make people dance again when he sees that the big band sound does not do it anymore. By accident, he stumbles on a new sound by Bill Haley and His Comets, who appear under their real name as a fictional small-town band, consisting of farmer boys turned amateur musicians. Thinking that this sound, labelled rock 'n' roll, could bring people to the dance floor and that the band could have nationwide success, Steve starts to plan his strategy. As he makes his plans, the narrative is interspersed with performances of songs by Bill Haley and His Comets as well as other groups of the time, which also maintain their real names in this fictional story. Obstacles in the form of a large talent agency that refuses to support them knock Hollis's plans back. Help, however, in the shape of real-life disc jockey and rock promoter Alan Freed (also appearing under his real name), comes to the rescue. He introduces the band at one of his music nights in a trendy night club and they are an immediate hit. Last-minute hiccups are easily overcome and the film finishes with the triumph of the music as part of a televised show as well as the formation of the couple, with Steve and Lisa Johns ([Lisa Gaye] a dancer with, and informal manager of, the band) getting married.

According to *Variety*, the film's production cost was approximately $300,000 (Arneel 1957: 4),[1] at a time when the average budget for a Hollywood studio-released feature was in the $1.3–1.5 million bracket[2] and when *Love Me Tender* (Webb), Elvis Presley's first film, released by Fox later in 1956, was produced on what was considered as 'a modest budget' of $1.25 million (Lev 2013: 180). *Rock around the Clock* was photographed in black and white stock at the time when over half of Hollywood productions (51% in 1955) were shot in Technicolor (Kindem 1979: 35). It had minimal location shooting and featured no film stars or even actors with a marquee value, with its main group of actors, Johnny Johnston, Alix Talton and Lisa Gaye having had a host of previous credits in Poverty Row B films in the 1940s and television series in the 1950s.

The film's producer, Sam Katzman, was one of the most established names in B film in the 1930s and 1940s, with a tenure in Poverty Row companies and major studios' B units, and had easily adapted to the new exploitation film model of the 1950s (see Chapter 2). Since 1946, and under a variety of company names, Katzman operated as an independent producer with a distribution contract with Columbia that enabled him to produce a large number of films per year (Dixon 2005: 48). Indicatively, alongside *RATC*, Katzman oversaw another 12 pictures released in 1956, all productions that fall under the exploitation rubric.

Six of these productions were also directed by *RATC* director, Fred F. Sears, who had started working with Katzman in the early 1950s on account of his ability to work quickly and efficiently, which he developed after a long tenure in B films and television shows. Finally, the film's duration was just 77 minutes, which made it a feature length film that could stand alone in theatres. Although B films in the 1930s and 1940s were routinely made with a duration of 60 minutes or even less, the arrival of television in the 1950s, with its cheap programming scheduled to fit within hour long slots, prompted low-budget filmmakers to elongate the duration of their pictures in order to be able to compete with the rival medium.

Given all these characteristics, it is not surprising that expectations were low. However, one additional, arguably fundamental, element that characterised exploitation film in the 1950s was its focus on an increasingly young audience demographic. Although 'young' is an age bracket that may include children, teenagers and young adults well into their thirties (Grant 1986: 199), in the 1950s the audience demographic that was exploitation filmmakers' primary target were teenagers. Indeed, Thomas Doherty identifies 'teenage audience' as the third of the three key elements of the exploitation film formula as a production strategy in the 1950s, with the other two being 'controversial, bizarre or timely subject matter amenable to wild promotion (exploitation)' and 'a substandard budget' (Doherty 1988: 8).

Taking this element too into consideration, *Rock around the Clock* emerges as a paradigmatic exploitation film in the mid-1950s. This is because it is the first film to target the teen demographic through exploiting rock 'n' roll, the music (and some of its connotations) most strongly associated with that audience at that particular moment in time, throughout the course of its narrative. Using the title of the most commercially successful record in that 'genre', 'Rock around the Clock' by Bill Haley and His Comets, and featuring the band together with other music groups of the time, both as part of the narrative and, especially, as performers of their hit songs, *RATC* had both a highly 'exploitable' title and 'a timely subject matter amenable to wild promotion', next to its 'substandard budget'.

Rock 'n' roll music had only emerged in the year prior to the film's release as an identifiable (and therefore marketable) category of music that was quickly embraced by White youth, while at the same time being branded as morally corrupting by adult institutions and assorted cultural custodians. With reports that the song 'Rock around the Clock' incited unruly behaviour in many young people who heard it as part of the opening and closing credits of major studio production

Blackboard Jungle (Brooks, 1955) and with popular media quick to associate the music with juvenile delinquency and other undesired manifestations of an emerging youth (sub)culture, it was no surprise that expectations for the film were not only low but also very specific. A low-budget picture by an exploitation film unit entitled *Rock around the Clock* and featuring the main band associated with this music was expected to stoke the fire of the rock 'n' roll controversy as this was played out in the country's media, most probably as a minor contributor destined to disappear after a few weeks in the theatres.

In many ways *RATC* confirmed these expectations but in other ways it confounded them. Its contribution to the rock 'n' roll controversy was made primarily through the title song reportedly inciting a similar unruly behaviour for some members of the audience, as *Blackboard Jungle* had done a year earlier, rather than through any representations of moral corruption and delinquency that were associated with the music and which featured heavily in the publicity and exploitation of other films of the time. Furthermore, despite its recent recuperation and canonisation, the film largely disappeared from popular culture, especially as the rock 'n' roll of the 1950s started to evolve into rock music in the 1960s and beyond. Within this context, the film's easily digestible and ahistorical chronicle of the emergence of rock 'n' roll made it irrelevant to debates about music and youth cultures, while its lowly exploitation film status meant that opportunities for re-releases were not many until the cable/video era of the 1980s.

On the other hand, *Rock around the Clock* did possess an element that most exploitation films of the time did not have, at least not in terms of the kind of *quality* that was evident in that film. That element was spectacle. Not related to exotic locations, panoramic vistas, or the use of widescreen technology that had been sweeping American cinema since the early 1950s, the spectacle of *RATC* was its musical performances, especially by the two main attractions of the film, Bill Haley and His Comets and The Platters. The two groups are seen performing in their entirety (though interrupted by narrative events) 11 songs in total, including chart-topping hits such as 'Rock around the Clock' (1954) and 'The Great Pretender' (1955), respectively, as well as other hit records such as 'See You Later, Alligator' (1956) and 'Only You' (1955). While similar exploitation films featured other major rock 'n' roll stars such as Fats Domino and Chuck Berry, none had performances of such major titles as *RATC*.

With rock 'n' roll only emerging as a distinct category of music in 1955 and with its associations with rhythm and blues (or R'n'B) and what was more broadly known as 'race music' still strongly scrutinised and debated, the presence in the film of bands like Bill Haley and His Comets and vocal groups like The Platters represented a unique opportunity for the millions of young people buying their records to see them perform their hit songs. Even more so as their appearance in the film was not in the form of background entertainment to support the narrative but, arguably, as the film's main attraction, around which the narrative was built. This is further emphasised both in the film's poster and the opening credits where the names of the bands appear before the names of the actors, and in the film's fictional universe where they maintain their real names. As a result, their musical performances, which took a very substantial part of the film's 77-minute duration, endowed *RATC* with a very particular form of spectacle that, arguably, helped it transcend its lowly exploitation origins and made it an unlikely commercial proposition in the world's theatres.

Indeed, despite the low expectations, the film proved wildly successful commercially. In the annual North American box-office table for 1956, *RATC* was cited in the (seemingly not particularly auspicious) 99th place out of 272 films produced by US companies in that year (Doherty 1995: 307), with a recorded box-office gross of $1.1 million (Arneel 1957: 4). This was much less than two studio-sponsored youth-focused films that did not (openly) go down the exploitation route: Warner Bros.'s *Rebel without a Cause* (Ray), which was released in 1955 but played in the theatres for most of 1956, and Fox's *Love Me Tender*, which found themselves in the 12th and 23rd place, respectively. Furthermore, 20th Century-Fox also released that year the exploitation title *Teenage Rebel* (Goulding), which landed on the 55th place, while another Katzman-produced film, *Earth vs. the Flying Saucers* (Sears) fared slightly better than *Rock around the Clock* – with a box-office gross of $1.25 million it reached the 85th place (ibid.).

It was, however, the film's international theatrical box-office performance that makes its commercial success close to phenomenal. Low-budget exploitation films tended to have very little marketing power outside the US where teen cultures were very different (and in many countries non-existent). Furthermore, many independent companies making such films did not have distribution offices outside the US and therefore had to license their films to local distributors who had the power to market them any way they wanted. However, as the success of rock 'n' roll music had quickly swept many countries around the world, *RATC* found itself in the envious position of exploiting subject matter that was not only topical but also truly international in its appeal. Furthermore, as *RATC* was represented around the world by the same distributor that had ushered it to commercial success in the

US, a Hollywood major with a global distribution network, the film's release abroad was handled with a similar level of marketing savvy, which enabled it to do exceptional business in international markets. Although worldwide box-office figures are always open to scrutiny given that there was no systematic auditing of international box office at that time, reports have ranged from citing a worldwide total of $2.4 million in early January 1957 (Arneel 1957: 4) to $4 million in early May 1957 ('$300,000 Picture's ...' 1957: 17). A later source brings the figure to $4.5 million (Barber 1962: 98), while the film's rentals from its world release were estimated at $3 million in February 1957 (Hammer 1957: 12). Even using the most conservative of these figures, $2.4 million represents an eight to one ratio of profit to cost (Doherty 1995: 307), which makes *RATC* justifiably 'one of the most spectacularly successful pictures of [that] year' (Arneel 1957: 4).

Such a commercial success prompted several other exploitation film companies such as American International Pictures, Vanguard Productions and Aurora Productions as well as exploitation film units in studios such as Universal to make their own rock 'n' roll films. However, this kind of success did not necessarily translate to cultural legitimacy for *RATC*. As we have mentioned already, the film's success at the global box office was not down to its story, its stars or its production values, elements that are important for a film's commercial performance and for attracting the attention of critics and industry that often translated to awards and cultural cachet. Indeed, at the top of the North American box office for that year, films such as *Guys and Dolls* (Mankiewicz), *The King and I* (Lang), *Trapeze* (Reed) and *High Society* (Walters) (at numbers 1 to 4, respectively) represented star-studded adaptations of Broadway productions and best-selling novels, shot in breath-taking widescreen technologies and glorious Technicolor, with budgets that ranged from $2.7 million (*High Society*) to $5.5 million (*Guys and Dolls*).[3] Together they grossed $31.5 million at the North American theatrical box office alone and received 15 Academy Award nominations.

Rock around the Clock, on the other hand, found success because it sold its audiences a spectacle consisting of revue-like musical performances of groups associated with rock 'n' roll music. It did that at a time when rock 'n' roll was emerging as a major music genre for young people in the US and internationally, and, importantly, had connotations of being responsible for morally corrupting teens by pandering to their baser instincts. In this respect, it is really significant that, despite a tame narrative that reimagined the emergence of the music by White rural (and completely erased the contribution of Black urban) America, *RATC* became primarily known for inciting unruly behaviour in young cinema patrons in the US and several other countries around the world. Echoing well-publicised (but arguably exaggerated) anecdotes that *Blackboard Jungle* had the same impact on young viewers who, on hearing the first notes of the song 'Rock around the Clock' during the film's opening credits, started to dance in the theatre aisles and cause other disturbances (Brode 2015: 14), the arrival of *RATC* in theatres was accompanied by similar reports.

However, the reports this time came primarily from other countries such as Norway, Belgium, West Germany, Australia and especially the UK, where the film's release in the autumn of 1956 coincided with the announcement of a 6-week UK tour by Bill Haley and His Comets in early 1957 ('Rock 'n' roll Riots ...' 1956: 1, 4). This means that the film did not have as strong an impact in the US in terms of inciting violence or other unruly behaviour. Some reports in cities such as Minneapolis, MN and La Crosse, WI mentioned riots and police intervention, while in Bridgeport, CT the film's screening was initially cancelled. However, according to the trade press of the time, most exhibitors had no problems with showing the film, although they did try to minimise the presence of 'high-pressure merchandizing' and other hard-selling tactics to avoid provoking trouble ('New "Rock" Explosion ...' 1956: 1; 'Col Finds Rowdy ...' 1956: 60). For this reason, although, as Thomas Doherty put it, 'American exhibitors were caught between desire for teenage dollars and dread of teenage violence' (1988: 83), when it came to *RATC*, they managed to negotiate a position whereby they got to avoid that violence while also cashing in on the rock 'n' roll craze.

The absence of serious incidents in American theatres may explain why the film did better box-office business internationally than in the US. It may also demonstrate why it was perceived as an insignificant contribution to the rock 'n' roll controversy of the mid-1950s and a minor addition to youth culture in the US. The film's cultural value seems to have been limited to its ability to excite teenagers and as a result no effort was made to address its textual qualities or its politics until well into the 1980s when academic criticism started to engage with it. In the process, the film was understood as a much more important proposition than was originally considered, while sophisticated analyses by scholars coming from film studies, popular music studies, dance studies, cultural studies and other academic disciplines have slowly canonised the film.

This volume builds on these studies by looking further at the film's impact on youth culture in the US and beyond through re-opening some areas of inquiry that have to do with its place in the American film industry and American cinema more broadly, while also introducing new ones that have to do with the ways in which it represents young people and lays bare the rules of commercial exploitation. Before we explain in more detail what each chapter will cover and the issues the volume will raise, the rest of this Introduction reviews the key scholarly work that engaged with *Rock around the Clock*.

Raising the Stakes: *Rock around the Clock* and Academic Criticism

The first sustained examination of the film, and the one that arguably exerted most influence in its understanding by the academic community, was by Thomas Doherty in his now classic study *Teenagers and Teenpics: The Juvenilization of American Movies in the 1950s* (1988; second edition, 2002).[4] The book places the emergence of the teen movie or teenpic as a distinct category of films within a complex context that was the product of developments in the film industry as well as in US society more broadly. At the core of this context Doherty identifies the widespread adoption by the industry of exploitation film practices, which, among the benefits they brought in terms of the studios keeping production and distribution costs in check, also proved effective in targeting an increasingly important teen audience (Doherty 1988: 3–10). Doherty explains how the decline of the studio system and classical Hollywood cinema more broadly, together with the rise of independent production, cinema's effort to compete with television, the impact of the conservative politics of the time and the emergence of a clearly defined teenage demographic (19–24) set the stage for the teenpic, which became a mainstay of exploitation filmmaking since the mid-1950s.

Doherty then identifies 'rock 'n' roll teenpics' as a sub-group within the broader teenpic category and dedicates a big chunk of his analysis to *RATC*. Starting from Sam Katzman's career as a filmmaker whose practices fit particularly well with the emergence of the exploitation film as it was establishing its presence across the industry, Doherty labels *RATC* a 'makeshift "quickie"' that nonetheless had the distinction of 'signall[ing] new production strategies [that] gave rise to a new kind of film: the teenpic' (Doherty 1988: 72). What is particularly distinctive about the film is that it 'became the first hugely successful film marketed to teenagers to the pointed exclusion of their elders' (74). Indeed, while its overall style and tone were not particularly different from previous Katzman films (77), its effort to target almost exclusively teen audiences made *RATC* an 'astonishing' box-office success (81), while also paving the way for an explosion of imitations and other types of exploitation teenpics (juvenile delinquency films, horror films and others). Key to this success was the film's title (80), which allowed Katzman, in true exploitation style, to build a story around the song and Bill Haley and His Comets who were contracted to appear in the film.

Doherty's focus remains primarily on the industrial impact of the film, though he also provides a brief analysis of its narrative and themes. Interestingly, he rejects the notion that the film's narrative is a 'mere filler' that sets up the numerous musical performances and argues that at the very least it acknowledges 'the subcultural ways of its target audience' and at most it validates them (Doherty 1988: 85). Indeed, he goes as far as to argue that a narrative analysis of this and other rock 'n' roll teenpics that does not take into consideration the question of validation and focuses only on the plot or the appreciation of performances misses the point of these films (98). For him, the emergence of the teenpic in the mid-1950s is as much about celebrating 'teenagers as a subcultural group' as it is about exploiting them as an audience.

Doherty's account has been critiqued for not acknowledging youth focused films before the 1950s (see Driscoll 2011: 27–44). In this book, we question the extent to which *Rock around the Clock* is a paradigmatic example of exploitation film when compared to both studio productions (such as *Blackboard Jungle*) and the low-budget films that imitated it (such as *Rock, Rock, Rock!* [Price, 1956]). As we argue in Chapter 3, the distinction between a major studio release and an exploitation film release (by a major studio or an independent company) is often not as clear cut. Conversely, there seem to be significant differences between exploitation films made by established industry practitioners who have distribution contracts with studios (such as Katzman) and small independent outfits that operate precariously at the very margins of the industry. Drawing on Brian Taves's taxonomy of B films (Taves 1995), we argue that *RATC*'s exploitation operates at a different level from that of many of its imitators, while its hybrid status as an independent production released by a Hollywood studio connects it also with major studio productions in ways that are perhaps more complex than those suggested by Doherty.

Two years after Doherty's volume, *RATC* became the subject of an article in the *Journal of Popular Culture*. Under the title 'Katzman's "Rock around the Clock": A Pseudo-historic Event' (Denisoff and Romanowski 1990), its authors examined the reports of riots that were allegedly incited by the film. Their research revealed that such reports were often exaggerated – 'dancing in the dimly lit aisles could hardly be termed riotous' (70) – which prompted them to question whether they should be part of the historiography of rock 'n' roll more broadly (77). Given their focus on questions of reception, Denisoff and Romanowski do not examine the film's textual details. However, it is the authors' careful consideration of the film's impact on its US youth audiences that makes this article an important source for approaching the film.

Through a close reading of various contemporaneous sources, the authors demonstrate how certain isolated incidents that took place during screenings of *RATC* and were reported in these publications were actually conflated with events that were *not* associated with the film. Indeed, incidents that were related to drinking or had happened *after* a rock 'n' roll concert were often retrospectively blamed to the music, contributing to a damning discourse that targeted any institution associated with rock 'n' roll (Denisoff and Romanowski 1990: 76). Furthermore, as the release of the film in March 1956 coincided with the publication of the interim report by the Senate Subcommittee to Investigate Juvenile Delinquency, which accused film (and the media more broadly) of having the power to trigger anti-social behaviour in teenagers, it is not surprising, they argue, that *Rock around the Clock* was perceived as an easy scapegoat (73).

Denisoff and Romanowski finish their article by calling all the '"troubles"' that were reported in the press as directly related to *RATC* in 1956 as '"pseudo-events,"' created by 'guardians of the public morality and special interest groups – ASCAP – [which] perceived a propitious opportunity to defeat the perverts of rock' (Denisoff and Romanowski 1990: 77). However, despite pointing the finger to financial interests (and not just to social factors that had to do with policing the nation's youth), they stop short of explaining how ASCAP (the American Society of Composers, Authors and Publishers), which represented the established record labels that tended not to focus on rock 'n' roll artists and music, was involved. On the other hand, the authors' suggestion that the swing era of the 1930s had already attracted objections similar to the ones raised in the rock 'n' roll era – 'subversion, racial integration, juvenile delinquency' (71) – and that overall swing may have had a lot more influence on rock 'n' roll and its representation on film than previously thought was taken up by Terry Monaghan's 'Rock around the Clock: The Record, the Film and the Last Historic Dance Revolt' (2008).

Monaghan's entry point is the dancing that accompanied rock 'n' roll music, which received much less critical attention than other elements related to it. He argues that the emerging (in the mid-1950s) rock 'n' roll music buckled a trend that wanted popular music made to be listened to rather than danced to and challenged dominant segregationist attitudes to the extent that it quickly became a social concern. With music stars such as Bill Haley and The Platters and leading rock 'n' roll disc jockey and promoter Alan Freed publicly expressing views about rock 'n' roll's potential for 'a more equal USA' (Monaghan 2008: 128), it is a historical moment that all these agents found themselves in this 'seminal' low-budget film (124). Monaghan then embarks on an analysis of the film's production culture by highlighting the Jewish immigrant status of Katzman and Freed and the extent to which it was mapped onto a strong tradition of entrepreneurialism that characterised the immigrant experience in the US throughout the 20th century and which often succeeded against dominant cultural norms (133–4).

In the case of *RATC*, the emphasis on cashing in on what was initially seen as a 'fad' through the means of a low-budget exploitation film meant that a space was created for an approach that privileged the 'quick buck' against a coherent ideological project enshrined in the institutional views of the studios and Hollywood at large (Monaghan 2008: 134). Katzman avoided the juvenile delinquency route that other exploitation films had taken, opting instead for the less risky strategy of treating rock 'n' roll as new music young people could dance to (ibid.). Going against contemporaneous trends that objected to youth dancing, Katzman looked at jitterbug and Lindy hop dancing that had been available since the 1930s and the swing era as a way to animate the music in the film (135–6). In doing this, he inadvertently tapped on the strong links that have existed between swing and the emerging rock 'n' roll music when it came to dancing (126–8) and therefore managed to capture some of the authentic elements of the rock 'n' roll music scene. As Monaghan puts it, *Rock Around the Clock* became 'the first and last rock 'n' roll exploitation movie to bring all these elements together as a composite artistic statement' (136). Of course, it is debatable that Katzman achieved all the above by design, with the use of jitterbug mainly designed to give the film a Broadway-style validation (Monaghan 2008: 137), while also ensuring that delinquency was marginalised (134–8). Still, by doing this he managed to capture rock 'n' roll's links to earlier youth music cultures, thus providing further context for understanding its presence in US society and culture at large.

Monaghan's article paved the way for further work that considers dancing as related to the film and rock 'n' roll music more broadly. However, his understanding of the concept of exploitation film and how *Rock around the Clock* fits this label seems unclear. On the one hand, he states that *RATC* 'utiliz[es] juvenile delinquent (J-D) movie's semi-confrontational style for its presentation of new teenage mores' (Monaghan 2008: 128) and sees it as an example of a 'confused genre' that uses 'Hollywood style sexual or delinquent cliches to the familiar visual norms of a segregationist perspective' (ibid.). On the other, he praises *RATC* for achieving an 'artistic representation of the rock 'n' roll music and dance business, *without a delinquent in sight*' (137; emphasis added). As mentioned above, questions about the film's exploitation status are addressed further in Chapters 2–4 of this book.

The next scholarly account to engage with the film in some detail was Amanda Ann Klein's *American Film Cycles: Reframing Genres, Screening Social Problems, and Defining Subcultures* (2011). Her discussion of *RATC* represents a section of a chapter focusing on the teenage film cycle of the mid-1950s to the early 1960s (122–4) and is another important contribution as she brings into the equation questions about the representation of subcultures and how they shape (and are shaped by) film cycles that operate within broader genre frameworks such as the youth film.

At the core of Klein's argument is the extent to which subcultures are 'complete' only when they have been reproduced through the recuperative powers of media companies – the film studios in the case of JD films, which, for Klein, represent a distinct film cycle in the 1950s and 1960s. As she argues, by the time such reproduction has taken place, both the subcultures and the studios can reap the benefits. The former are able to disseminate their 'to-be-looked-at-ness' to large audiences and therefore confirm their subcultural status, which relies largely on the visibility of their style (Klein 2011: 104). The latter are able to make money out of projecting that visibility but also, significantly, play a part in shaping that subculture as they hold the means of representation and therefore can further refine (and often define) the subculture style for a broader audience (105–6).

Writing specifically about *Rock around the Clock*, Klein mentions how watching the film could help audiences learn the latest dance steps and goes as far as to argue that the film's *raison d'être* was to present extended scenes of teenage subcultural styles. Furthermore, by introducing the rock 'n' roll subculture through the adult perspective of manager Steve Hollis, who initially does not know how to label it or understand the slang its members use, *RATC* automatically validates the teen subculture and its codes as distinct from the dominant culture represented by Steve (Klein 2011: 123), an argument that harks back to Doherty (1988: 98).

Although Klein's argument is convincing, it is unclear why she labels *Rock around the Clock* a JD teenpic (a juvenile-delinquent-themed teenpic) (Klein 2011: 123, 129), effectively equating all subcultural activity with juvenile delinquency, when the film in question displays subcultural activity *without* any references to violence or crime. Such an assumption also weakens one of her suggestions about how JD films contain teenage threat, when she cites *RATC* as an example of a JD film in which 'teenagers' delinquent behavior is shown to be innocent and harmless after all' (129). Although such a resolution stands for films that followed *RATC* such as *Shake, Rattle and Rock!* (Cahn, 1956) and *Don't Knock the Rock* (Sears, 1956), the absence of any form of delinquency from *RATC* means that any implications that rock 'n' roll is 'harmless' are framed from rather different perspectives; ones that showcase how it will not threaten the cultural industries and the taste hierarchies they produce. As we argue in Chapter 1, *Rock around the Clock* promotes a different type of subculture, one more closely aligned with the category of the 'cultural rebel' than the 'juvenile delinquent' (Brake 1985).

Paul N. Reinsch's 'Music over Words and Sound over Image: "Rock Around the Clock" and The Centrality of Music in Post-Classical Film Narration' (2013) revisits questions of dancing and rock 'n' roll to explore the extent to which *RATC* and *Blackboard Jungle* represent rare examples of films in which sound dominates the image. He suggests that the use of the song 'Rock around the Clock' invites the audience to listen to the music and respond to it by dancing rather than watch the film and concentrate on its narrative (8). As a result, the two films that carry this song challenge the conventions of spectatorship as these are embedded in theatre architecture and the kind of engagement it encourages audiences to have with films on screen.

Of the two films, Reinsch finds *RATC* the more radical proposition. While *Blackboard Jungle*'s use of 'Rock around the Clock' provided a rhythm to the first introduction of rock 'n' roll on film, encouraged audiences to focus more on recorded music rather than narrative and through its lyrics invited audiences to dance and therefore alter their relationship to the screen (Reinsch 2013: 7–10), *RATC* took all these elements further. This is not only because it included performances of the title and other songs throughout the film but also because these performances were reproduced from their original recordings. In doing this, it addressed its audience both as listeners and as viewers, altering further their relationship to cinema (12–13). Furthermore, with Katzman also paying particular attention to dancing, as a key aspect of the film's narrative is about demonstrating rock 'n' roll to the younger generation and making America dance again, the audience for that film has yet another reason to add dancing to the range of their potential responses to the film (15).

Reinsch also makes another important point when he argues that films with a sketchy narrative that tend to be dominated by musical performances often find these performances adding complexity to the narrative. Focusing especially on montage sequences that show the rise of rock 'n' roll through images of recordings, club live shows, dancing and trade press headlines, which are edited under the sound and lyrics of 'Rock around the Clock', he argues that they exceed the requirements of the narrative and function as a means to help rock 'n' roll become a 'mass culture' (Reinsch 2013: 16). Equally importantly, such sequences help reclaim the music from its ties to violence and juvenile delinquency, while at the same time engaging in dialogue with a variety of texts and media that legitimate the music further and present the road to success for the most famous song and performer of that era (17). This is a point that we examine in more detail but from a different prism when we consider the film as an (exploitative) cinematic adaptation of the song that gives the film its title in Chapter 4.

The one discordant note in Reinsch's account is the claim that the 'unoriginal' narrative of *RATC* was based on *Orchestra Wives* (Mayo, 1942), 'a Glenn Miller film where he is the Bill Haley-like purveyor of new sounds' (2013: 14). Although the latter film opens with Miller's trademark music and includes musical performances in quick succession, the two narratives otherwise have few lines of contact. At no point does Miller (who plays a bandleader under the fictional name Gene Morrison) present his work as new or struggle to have it accepted by the public, while the rest of the story focuses much more on the band being on tour and the impact this has on the wives of the musicians. If anything, it is *The Glenn Miller Story* (Mann, 1954) that is arguably closer to the spirit of *Rock around the Clock*. Here the narrative revolves around Miller trying to break into the music business through unusual musical arrangements that initially prevent him from success, and it is equally dispersed with performances of some of his greatest hits. However, that picture is a conventional biopic, while *RATC* has no (direct) aspirations to capture Haley's life and career, even though he appears in the film under his real name. In this respect, *RATC* seems to be closer to the 'jukebox musical' format that David E. James examines in detail.

In his book *Rock 'n' Film* (2016), James provides a detailed definition of this term:

> Jukebox musicals gave rhythm and blues and other early rock 'n' roll a wide social audibility, visibility, and publicity, bringing to the whole nation a cultural development founded on regional black

music and dance. Their fundamental attraction was the audio-visual spectacle of the stars as they lip-synced to their current or recent hit records, which provided an opportunity to hear them or see them, respectively, over a theatrical sound system much louder that a domestic record player and in a larger-than-life unob-structed theatrical projection, and perhaps even to dance along with them.

(James 2016: 43)

For James, *RATC* is the film that paved the way for this phenomenon, though he also provides a fascinating analysis of the film's narrative and style, showcasing levels of innovation and complexity that belie its lowly exploitation status. For instance, he is quick to point out how the film 'renovat[ed] the conventions of the classic show musical' as it followed its structure of combining the spectacle of music and dance within a fictional narrative world (35). In this case, however, it is only the performances and not the lyrics that are 'integrated into the diegetic world and propel the plot' (ibid.), which separates such films from the classic Hollywood musical. The two main protagonists (Steve and Lisa) represent different aspects of cultural industries and possess different skills, which in the end combine to provide a solution to a problem: overcome (the little) industrial and social resistance to rock 'n' roll music and develop an institutional context within which this music and the youth culture it is linked with are accepted (35–6).

But where, arguably, the film is even more radical than that is in its privileging of discourses (or 'motifs' as James calls them) of media management and media industrial and institutional contexts as the key means through which rock 'n' roll can be engaged with, can be contained and, ultimately, can be exploited (James 2016: 37). James starts this argument by acknowledging the important role of dancing in the film and its narrative, to the extent that it often dominates musical performances. This emphasis on dancing (and Lisa's role in it) both propels the plot and helps resolve its ideological problems: rock 'n' roll as a music to dance to makes it palatable for the establishment to accept it as a new sound and helps it achieve recognition, while Lisa and Steve, who promote this from their respective gendered positions as a dancer and a manager, end up married (39–40).

However, the film's main protagonist, James correctly asserts, is Steve, and it is his actions as a manager that are instrumental in legitimating rock 'n' roll. He is the one who identifies that people have stopped dancing (and in the process have been missing an opportunity for the exuberant celebration of community and energy that dancing celebrates); he is the one who decides to do something about it; he is the one who correctly assesses the need to turn Bill Haley and His Comets from amateurs to professionals if they want to achieve success; he is connected to booking offices, he can arrange television networks to cover events and he is friends with radio and promotion industry top professional Alan Freed who at the right moment can be counted to provide his support (James 2016: 41). *RATC*, James argues, 'recognizes that rock 'n' roll originated with the vernacular performance of rural, socially marginal youthful amateurs' (though this is a very partial and ideologically suspect recognition that erases the racial dimension of the emergence of rock 'n' roll), 'rather than the established show business industry'. However, he continues, 'it fulfils itself only when an adult professional takes over its management and administers it as a component of existing industrial culture, simultaneously renewing and consolidating its integrated structures' (ibid.). Not at all bad for a lowly exploitation film from a producer who oversaw another 12 titles that year alone.

James's and all other scholarly accounts in this section clearly demonstrate the film's importance as a text that engages with the emergence of rock 'n' roll music in complex and multifaceted ways. They also respond in the strongest possible way to non-critical views that dismiss the film's value and perpetuate its perception as unworthy of serious examination as was the case with Jim Dawson, who wrote that the film 'set a low standard for Hollywood's treatment of rock 'n' roll' (Dawson 2005: 155). If anything, these scholarly accounts provide a strong counter view that has been working steadily to legitimate a film that 68 years since its release has all but been forgotten by popular culture. This book will continue this project and the last section will briefly outline how it will do it.

The Chapters

Chapter 1 starts with examining the social, economic and political contexts that gave rise to the main audience for teenpics such as *RATC*, namely the teenager. We argue that the teenager is a reimagining of the broader term 'youth' at a particular moment in time (the mid-1950s), to which rock 'n' roll, with its connotations of delinquency and crime, provided a powerful imaginary. We then embark on a survey of how American cinema contributed to the trajectory of this reimagining by looking at key films of the first half of the 1950s and the extent to which they portrayed young people immersed in subcultural activities that more often than not were linked to juvenile delinquency. With such predecessors, it is interesting that *RATC* buckles this trend on a textual level. As we argue in the final section of the chapter, in representing rock 'n' roll youth as a subculture, *RATC* draws more on the subcultural category of the 'cultural rebel' than that of the 'delinquent', and therefore invites a different kind of analysis than the one offered by much of the existing literature.

Chapter 2 examines the production of *RATC* as an example of exploitation film. It starts with a summary of an industry in transition, with the so-called B film of the 1930s and 1940s giving way to new low-budget formulas in the 1950s that became known as exploitation film, before turning its attention to Sam Katzman. Having produced over 100 B films in Poverty Row studios, Katzman became a key figure in this transition to exploitation film. The chapter discusses Katzman's filmmaking practices, demonstrating how making teenpics was an extension of approaches to filmmaking that were routine in his operations as a producer. It ends with a detailed analysis of *RATC* as an exploitation film production, focusing primarily on how Katzman 'exploited' the song 'Rock around the Clock' as the origin for the film and as the cornerstone for the distribution approach he developed together with Columbia Pictures, the film's distributor.

As we have already indicated, *RATC*'s status as an 'exploitation' film is not as stable as it has been suggested, and Chapter 3 examines this argument in detail. Specifically, it contextualises the production and distribution of the film by demonstrating how they converge with and diverge from a major studio production such as *Blackboard Jungle* and low(er)-end independent productions such as *Shake, Rattle and Rock!* and *Rock, Rock, Rock!*. The ensuing analysis shows that the exploitation film terrain may be a more slippery category than what has been presented, and require a more nuanced approach than the ones afforded to it, in existing literature. We argue that *RATC* stands out from the cycle of other low-budget rock 'n' roll films that followed it, while even major film productions like *Blackboard Jungle* that inspired it may be seen as examples of exploitation cinema. Drawing on Brian Taves's work on B-film production (1995), the chapter ends with proposing a taxonomy of exploitation filmmaking in the 1950s and demonstrating where *RATC* fits in such a scheme.

Chapter 4 examines how the exploitative practices of the film's production translate into the film's narrative, style and themes. By analysing the stylistic and narrative choices the filmmakers made we argue that the film 'packages' a very particular and non-threatening rock 'n' roll youth (sub)culture that stands at odds with dominant representations of youth in mainstream US media as dangerous, delinquent and transgressive. This positive image of rock 'n' roll also helps this kind of music and culture break further into a White middle class youth demographic and increase record sales, especially as it dissociates music and culture from their Black origins, both musically and geographically. Behind this 'simplistic package', however, lies a complex and highly self-reflexive media text that at its core is about the 'art of exploitation'. Whether this is articulated through an effort to 'adapt' a song into a film, through a narrative that lays bare the rules of exploitation in the media industries or through utilising existing dancing styles to sell the music, *RATC* operates in an exploitation film sector that is not as monolithic as it may be assumed to be. Indeed, such a sector occasionally allows films with significant complexity and innovative vigour to transcend that status and find commercial success and scholarly acclaim as is the case with *RATC*.

The book closes with a coda in which we note the film's place in contemporary popular culture, focusing primarily on the ways it has influenced, rather surreptitiously, 1980s youth films, in particular *Dirty Dancing* (Ardolino, 1987). As we argue, *RATC* has a great affinity with *Dirty Dancing*, not only because both films present a new form of dancing (for White middle class young people) as a validation of a particular (Black) music, but also because they are examples of independent film production with roots in the exploitation sector as well as titles that did unexpectedly well at the box office internationally.

In doing all this work, the book will continue the legitimation project of this 'deceptively complex' youth film, while also contributing to youth film research and its links to exploitation cinema.

Notes

1 Other sources bring the film's budget higher, at approximately $500,000 (Haley 1957: 9), but even with this figure the film would be deemed a big hit, its box-office gross being five times its budget.
2 These figures are cited as the production budget range for MGM films in the 1949–54 period ('The American Film Industry ....' n.d.)
3 For details of these films' budgets, see their respective pages in the Internet Movie Database (www.imdb.com).
4 Doherty also presented a distillation of this work as part of a chapter under the title 'Exploitation Teenpics, 1955–1957: A Study of Exploitation Filmmaking' (1995) for a collection on the Hollywood studio system.

1   (Re)imagining Youth

The 'Birth' of the Teenager under the Spectre of Rock 'n' Roll

On 4 January 1954 *Life* magazine published an article on US youth under the telling title 'The Luckiest Generation'. The article was illustrated heavily with photos of American youth engaged in both serious/work related activities, ranging from doing homework and acquiring work skills to investing their savings, and light/leisure related ones, from listening to records to attending formal and informal dances. In no uncertain terms, *Life* showed a happy, confident cohort that was bound together by age, that was aware of its place in society and that shared interests, attitudes and styles as these could be seen in their dressing codes and hair styles, in the places they tended to congregate and in their penchant for listening to music and dancing. As the anonymous writer of the article explained:

> Young people 16 to 20 are the beneficiaries of the very economic collapse that brought chaos almost a generation ago. The Depression tumbled the nation's birth rate to an all-time low in 1933, and today's teenage group is proportionately a smaller part of the total population than in more than 70 years. Since there are fewer of them, each – in the most prosperous time in U.S. history – gets a bigger piece of the nation's economic pie than any previous generation ever got.
> ('The Luckiest Generation' 1954: 27)

Such images and the discourses surrounding them were in abundance in US popular media of the time. As Steven Tropiano asserts, these were the years of the 'affluent society', when 'the size of the middle class grew' and 'more Americans were taking home a bigger paycheck' (Tropiano 2006: 18–19). This included the younger generation who 'had extra money in their pockets to spend on *really* important "stuff" like Elvis's latest single, dungarees, poodle skirts, makeup, jewelry, *Vault of Horror* comics, and, of course, the movies' (19; emphasis in the original).

DOI: 10.4324/9781315544908-2

On the other hand, such images also constituted a very partial representation of teenage life. Not surprisingly for the times, they ignored completely the teenage experience of African American and other ethnic minority groups in US society that were largely excluded from the 'bigger piece of the nation's economic pie' that their White counterparts were benefitting from. Second, they tended to present a rather unrealistic picture of 'working youth', with the relevant photos in the *Life* article celebrating more young people's proximity to commodities and the money they make rather than their experience as working youths. Finally, taking the *Life* magazine pictures as representative of such images, it is clear that they celebrate a middle-class youth in their late teens that is very 'adult like' in its orientation and cultural conduct, dressed in tuxedos and ball gowns, and enjoying drinking, dining and dancing that requires a lot more than just disposable income from pocket money and part time jobs. It also means that early teens, much more dependent on family and adult institutions, and lacking the freedom and economic independence of later ages, are also not part of this picture.

Perhaps more intriguingly, the *Life* article does not include any references to juvenile delinquency, youth gang membership, hot rodding and other subcultural activities that have also been synonymous with the 1950s but did not fit the 'luckiest generation' script. Such activities, of course, have been intricately linked with the emergence of rock 'n' roll a year later, in 1955, which became an overarching discourse through which teen culture would be defined for the rest of the decade. As Cynthia Rose put it:

> In the public mind, the adjective 'teenage' referred to leisure, pleasure and conspicuous consumption. The teenagers' new music, rock'n'roll, symbolized a world of youth, caught up momentarily in hedonism and unrelated to adult interests. Rock'n'roll also brought with it a host of concepts and images that fired the public's ideas of youth: delinquency, adolescent gangs, motorcycle worship, ballroom-dance halls, jazz clubs, Melody Bars, Teddy Boys and similar phenomena. Parents feared [...] [as] early rock'n'roll was aggressive in providing ideas of style that were exclusively teenage.
>
> (Rose 1980: 841)

What is problematic in such an account, however, is that juvenile delinquency, teen gangs and other youth subcultural activities pre-existed the rock 'n' roll era. Indeed, eight months before the publication of the *Life* magazine article, on 27 April 1953, the Judiciary Committee of the United States Senate created a Special Subcommittee on Juvenile Delinquency to investigate the causes of this phenomenon, paying particular attention to the role of mass media in influencing the nation's youth ('Congress Investigates ...' n.d.; Gilbert 1986: 144). Furthermore, previous decades had seen similar concerns (and debates on how to address them), with images of the flapper in the 1920s raising questions of 'wild adolescence and youth run amuck' (quoted in Shary 2005: 6) and the unemployed youth of the Depression in the 1930s (as exemplified by the young boys in the film *Dead End* [Wyler, 1937]) having made a notable impression. Gilbert asserts that juvenile delinquency in the US had already become an 'important issue' in 1942 and 1943 (Gilbert 1986: 25), with the latter year also having seen the publication of sociologist William Foote Whyte's classic *Street Corner Society*. This was a study of the social life worlds of street gangs or, more specifically, the 'corner boys' (a group of young men 'who center their activities upon particular street corners' [Whyte 1943: xviii]).

However, for a number of critics the 1950s had arguably witnessed a dramatic shift in these concerns given the extent to which the cohort in question represented a 'historical entity', that was 'exceptional in its size and wealth, but perhaps most importantly, in its self-awareness as a unified generation' (Brickman 2014: 32). This self-awareness was reinforced by adult institutions, with Amanda Ann Klein arguing that for the first time, 'teenagers were informed, on a mass scale, that they were separate, special, and different from mainstream adult society – and were told so by that very same adult society' (Klein 2011: 111), and Thomas Doherty noting how 'their social position as teenagers was carefully nurtured and vigorously reinforced by adult institutions around them' (Doherty 1988: 46). In this respect, it comes as no surprise that discourses about delinquency and crime were also magnified, especially as they circulated in increasingly mediated forms, which often represented highly distorted views of the realities of the time (Shary 2005: 20).

And yet for many scholars who have examined youth cultures in 1950s America as well as popular critics (such as Cynthia Rose who appears above), juvenile delinquency is intricately linked with rock 'n' roll, which nonetheless did not make its impact in popular culture felt until 1955, halfway into the decade. Indeed, *Life* magazine would also be there to capture that 'moment' through the article 'Rock 'n Roll: A Frenzied Teen-age Music Craze Kicks up a Big Fuss' [*sic*] that was published on 18 April 1955. This time the images were more unsettling than in the earlier issue, connoting frenzy and chaos, with photos depicting large numbers of young people gathered to see bands and dance – with Black youth now visible and Black performers entertaining mixed race audiences. Not surprisingly, the article starts with a

story about (and a picture of) the New Haven, CT police chief who
had banned rock 'n' roll parties in his town ('Rock 'n Roll: A Frenzied
...' 1955: 166–8) and continues by highlighting rock 'n' roll's links to
'race music' which, although accurate, would help stoke the fire of
controversy further given the magazine's wide (and White) readership.

It is clear then that American teenagers as defined by their participation in subcultural activities pre-existed the emergence of rock 'n'
roll. However, rock 'n' roll gave such activities a powerful new imaginary that almost instantly overshadowed the (arguable) positivity surrounding youth in the earlier half of the decade. Young people
continued to benefit from the 'affluent society' in the latter half of the
1950s but their relationship to the adult world shifted abruptly. Rather
than continue to be moulded in the values and principles of the previous generation, Timothy Shary writes, 'they embraced the fast-paced,
energetic rock tunes as a way to rebel, to distinguish themselves from
the staid styles of their predecessors, and to sublimate their sexual
urges' (Shary 2005: 18). Subcultural activities such as drag racing,
gang membership, use of slang, adoption of a particular dress code
and others found immediately a soundtrack and an attitude that not
only helped define them as such but, equally importantly, helped spec-
tacularise them further, to the extent that their presence became particularly noted by the media and informed a larger moral panic about
the state of the nation's youth.

It is within this context that the teenager was 'born' in the mid-
1950s. Spectacularly visible and therefore clearly identifiable across
gender and even some race lines, teenagers became instantly commodified, with rock 'n' roll becoming the lynch pin for a number of cultural industries to organise their production lines with that consumer
group in mind. Music, film, fashion, print, leisure – they all provided a
formidable array of products and services that structured teenagers'
spending habits, while more traditional sectors such as the automotive
industry courted the teenage dollar more long-term. According to
Tropiano, by 1953, young people's disposable income was calculated to
be in the region of $9 billion (Tropiano 2006: 20), while by 1957 the
youth market was reported to be worth $30 billion (quoted in Mundy
1999: 98). The moral panic ushered by the arrival of rock 'n' roll was
also good for business and the nation's economy more broadly.

From Generic Youth to Spectacular Teens

This reimagining of youth as teenagers under the spectre of rock 'n' roll
can be seen clearly if one compares films focusing on young people in

the pre-rock 'n' roll era against ones made after it. Interestingly, the early years of the decade are almost completely bereft of films focusing specifically on the lives and cultures of young people. Even the few examples that exist tend to be low-budget B films coming outside the Hollywood studios from companies such as Monogram. Titles such as *Hot Rod* (Collins, 1950) and *The Rose Bowl Story* (Baudine, 1952) bring to the screen stories about subcultural activities such as participating in illegal car racing and college football, respectively. However, despite its emphasis on the young and the depiction of their subcultural lifestyles, the 59-minute long *Hot Rod* is much closer in spirit to the B films of the 1940s than the exploitation films that would become dominant in the 1950s (see Chapter 2). On the one hand, its upbeat orchestral music score (that becomes particularly prominent in the scene when the young protagonist starts building his hot rod) undermines any efforts towards representing an authentic subcultural moment. On the other, any subcultural activities involving young people and hot rodding by the end of the film become easily institutionalised, with the young cohort happily agreeing to do racing against the clock and under the supervision of adult organisers rather than racing illegally against each other. As for *The Rose Bowl Story*, which was a rare Monogram film shot in colour, despite the presence of young Natalie Wood, the emphasis is too much on the importance of the institution of the Rose Bowl Game to make it a legitimate film about collegiate youth subcultures.

In this context, when *The Wild One* (Benedek, 1953) appeared in December 1953, it seemed to have come out of nowhere. Released by Hollywood major Columbia Pictures, the film was produced by top-rank independent producer Stanley Kramer's production company and was directed by László Benedek, who had previously helmed both studio productions and television shows. However, its black and white cinematography and its rather short duration of 79 minutes also suggest a relatively low-budget effort, despite the fact that it starred Marlon Brando, who had come to this film after his triumphant, Academy Award nominating turns in *A Streetcar Named Desire* (Kazan, 1951) and *Viva Zapata!* (Kazan, 1952).

In true exploitation style, *The Wild One* opens with an intertitle framing the events that would follow as shocking and in need of inciting a response from audiences so that they will not happen in reality. This then gives way to a voiceover by main character Johnny Strabler (Marlon Brando), who frames further the upcoming narrative events as preventable. However, he also admits that he did not do anything to stop these events, which he calls a 'mess', despite the fact that his meeting with a girl impacted the way he felt about his role in the whole incident. The end of the voiceover, which takes place over a static shot of an open road coincides with the passing through of a motorcycle gang, its members dressed in black leather and sporting hats and sunglasses as they cruise confidently on their bikes led by Johnny (see Figure 1.1).

The 'mess' that Johnny refers to in his voiceover is an escalation of a number of incidents that take place in a small California town, when Johnny's Black Rebels Motorcycle Club gang arrives in it and interrupts the quiet routine of its inhabitants. At the beginning, the Black Rebels seem to be rowdy but harmless. However, once a rival motorcycle gang arrives in the same town, things quickly spiral out of control. A group of townsfolk decide to take the law in their own hands by kidnapping Johnny who manages to escape on his motorbike. Chased by them he is thrown off it, with the bike moving a few more metres, enough to run over an old man who dies instantly. As the whole town is ready to fight against the bikers, a strong police force arrives in time to stop the events from escalating further. Johnny is arrested and

Figure 1.1 Johnny Strabler and the Black Rebels Motorcycle Club on their way to make a 'mess' in *The Wild One*

threatened with a long time in prison, before last minute testimonies convince the sheriff that he was not responsible for the death of the old man. The bikers are then ordered to leave town and never come back. Johnny, however, does come back on his own, acknowledging his feelings for a girl he met at the town café and, potentially, his intention for a return to a lawful life.

As it is evident from the above summary, *The Wild One* has few points of contact with issues directly related to teen culture. Generically, it falls under the crime drama category, which was a major production trend in the late 1940s and early 1950s, when the industry wide adoption of location shooting practices helped enhance such films' quest for realism. At the end of the film, the law establishes order again, while the main protagonist/criminal redeems himself, which allows for narrative closure even if the main problem (in this case motorcycle gang violence) remains. Furthermore, the members of the gang are all decidedly adults, which removes the film further from any notions of juvenile delinquency or youth cultures. Additionally, the score for the film was based on jazz compositions that had become a staple of Hollywood productions in the 1950s, even though, as Peter Stanfield has convincingly argued, jazz had continued to have a strong presence in teenpics, despite the fact that rock 'n' roll songs tended to attract most attention (Stanfield 2015: 90, 104).

However, it is the film's focus on the motorcycle gang as a subculture with its own dress code, style, slang and flexible moral compass that has made it stand out in the history of youth cinema. As Jay Scott put it, '*The Wild One* was a movie about a subculture with potential' (Scott 1983: 33) that could be understood in different ways by its audiences, which included young people. One of the most celebrated scenes in the film involves Johnny responding to the question of what he is rebelling against. 'Whaddaya got?', Johnny replies, with the camera switching from a medium shot to a close-up of Brando's face, emphasising the weight of his response. Furthermore, as he does not provide any examples of what he is rebelling against, he effectively asks audiences to come up with their own list. As a result, Scott continues, although *The Wild One* was not a film that targeted a youth audience and although Brando was almost 30 years old, teenagers of the time did adopt him as an icon 'for what leaked out around the edges of the tightly moralistic stor[y] in which [he] was trapped – getting around constrictions was something teens knew a bit about' (32).

Given the absence of direct focus on young people, it is not surprising that *The Wild One* did not establish a new trend or prompt similar films. Indeed, there seems to be a gap of over a year between that film and *Blackboard Jungle*, the next important film for youth cultures at the time, which was released on 19 March 1955. That was the exact time when rock 'n' roll was breaking into the mainstream, and *Blackboard Jungle* benefitted immensely from this coincidence given its filmmakers' decision to use 'Rock around the Clock' in its opening and closing credits. Although we provide a detailed discussion of this film in Chapter 3 in relation to exploitation filmmaking, we highlight here the extent to which *Blackboard Jungle* equates youth subcultural activities to juvenile delinquency, with both being framed from the start by rock 'n' roll music.

Like *The Wild One*, *Blackboard Jungle* opens with an intertitle that highlights that it will represent disturbing incidents. However, unlike the earlier film, it reveals from the start the nature of the problem – juvenile delinquency in schools – while also reassuring the viewer that the events depicted are fictional. As soon as the intertitle starts to fade out and the opening credits start to roll, 'Rock around the Clock' begins to play, effectively providing the soundtrack for the stated problem. More than that, the song continues to play after the credits and into the opening scene which shows young boys dance to it in a school yard as Mr Dadier (Glenn Ford), a schoolteacher, arrives in this deprived-looking, inner-city neighbourhood to be interviewed for a teaching post. The song's ambiguous status – it started as non-diegetic sound but has now become diegetic as the dancing students seem to be able to hear it (Reinsch 2013: 6) – immediately draws attention to it as a major framing device (see Figure 1.2). For Reinsch, it 'visualize[s] rock' by 'provid[ing] a rhythm and suggest[ing] some of the aggression to come' (ibid.). Equally importantly, 'the song's energy and insistent rhythm overwhelm the film's visual address and potentially draw the audience's attention away from the screen entirely' (ibid.), which goes a long way to explain the reports of youth dancing in the aisles that have become synonymous with the film.

Reinsch's argument also goes a long way to explain the transformative power of rock 'n' roll in the reimagining of youth – here in the shape of teenage high school students who seem to be heading to a life of delinquency, if not already being members of gangs. Of course, what is interesting is that this trajectory would have taken place whether it was framed by rock 'n' roll or not. The novel on which the film was based was published in the spring of 1954, with MGM purchasing the film rights in April of that year (see Chapter 3). Furthermore, the events represented in book and film were reportedly based on the novel's author Evan Hunter's personal experience as a teacher in an inner-city school that took place several years earlier, in 1950 (Matthews 1984: E-8). It is clear then that

Figure 1.2 Non-diegetic rock 'n' roll spills out to the narrative and is visualised by dancing teens in *Blackboard Jungle*

rock 'n' roll has nothing to do with the problem of juvenile delinquency and its manifestation in the nation's school system. Indeed, up until the autumn of 1954, when the film was still in production, rock 'n' roll – which had yet to break through to the mainstream – was not part of the film's production design. Richard Brooks's script included a note that stated that 'as modern jazz enters the daily life and speech patterns of today's youth in America, this film will be scored entirely with jazz, swing, blues and sentimental ballads' (quoted in Reinsch 2013: 9), which reinforces Stanfield's point about the links between jazz and teen subcultures. However, the filmmaker later decided to add rock on the list and included a hand-written reference to the 78 r.p.m. 'Rock around the Clock' (ibid.) which had only been released a few months earlier, in April 1954, without any commercial success.

As will be discussed in more detail in Chapter 3, the news of the inclusion of 'Rock around the Clock' in *Blackboard Jungle* was only announced in late January 1955, less than two months before its US theatrical release. This suggests that the decision to include the song was most likely taken during the film's post-production but mostly during the month when reports about the breakthrough of rock 'n' roll to the mainstream were increasing in numbers. Still, the rest of the film was scored primarily through jazz pieces, with rock 'n' roll music limited only to the opening and closing credits (and part of the opening scene), but effectively bookmarking the film and assuming responsibility for its content. This included numerous scenes of teenage subcultural activities, such as gang membership, use of slang, dress code, as well as criminal activities such as vandalism, the use of physical violence and attempted rape. On the other hand, the adult perspective to the events as represented through Dadier's narrative agency and the teacher-as-saviour narrative trope represent a rather conventional film that is elevated by the significant role of a young Sidney Poitier, who as a black teen student with strong leadership skills helps the teacher win the class and excise the bad elements.

Despite this conventionality, and as was the case with *The Wild One, Blackboard Jungle* also allowed young audiences to 'read oppositionally', to 'read like teenagers', even though primarily it invited audiences to 'read as adults' (Medovoi 2005: 139, 146, 140). From using 'Rock around the Clock' to prompt viewers to identify with the multiracial student cohort rather than the White adult Dadier (158), to cultivating an emasculated image for the teacher while masculinising the students (157), the film provides ample opportunities for identification with the delinquent youth. 'If *Blackboard*'s significance had been exhausted by [its adult-targeting] "social problem" meanings', Medovoi asserts, 'it would never have become a textual prototype for the teenpic' (146). It is clear that rock 'n' roll, in the shape of 'Rock around the Clock', was extremely important in helping the film 'speak' to teenagers when the rest of its 'language' was by and large adult.

Before closing this section with a discussion of *Rebel without a Cause*, the last important film in the reimaging of youth as teenagers, we briefly note the contribution of two other titles, *Teen-Age Crime Wave* (Sears, 1955) and *Running Wild* (Biberman, 1955). Both were decidedly low-budget exploitation films that were released through the Hollywood majors (Columbia and Universal, respectively). The former represents one of the earliest uses of the word 'teen-age' in a film title. It is also a Sam Katzman production that was directed by Fred F. Sears and was released in the autumn of 1955 just a few months before they teamed up again for *RATC*. The latter is a seldom discussed film about delinquent youth that nonetheless has the honour of having featured the first full rendition of a rock 'n' roll song as part of its narrative, Bill Haley and His Comets' 'Razzle Dazzle', and introduced a jitterbug-inspired rock 'n' roll dancing that *RATC* would elaborate further. Together with *Rebel without a Cause*, these films were released within the space of one month (November–December 1955) and provide a clear throughline for understanding the 'birth of the teenager' in the mid-1950s.

Taking more than one cue from *Blackboard Jungle, Teen-Age Crime Wave* also starts with an intertitle suggesting that it is a film about juvenile delinquency. But rather than concentrate on its impact on the education system, here it is on the 'social system' more broadly. The prologue also labels the events fictional but that they could take place in any city, inviting audiences to take measures to stop them from happening. The film then opens with a young girl in a bar being picked up by an older man. On the way to her house, two young men attack the older man and steal his money, revealing that the girl had acted as a bait for criminal activity. The police, however, arrives on time and captures the girl as well as another young female who had found herself amid this setup without knowing it. The two girls end up in a juvenile facility but when they are moved to another prison, the young men ambush the car, kill the policeman driving it and hide in a farm until they come up with a plan to escape to Mexico. In the farm they brutalise the old owners and their son who comes to visit them. But the police, accompanied by the innocent girl's father, quickly tracks them down. In the ensuing chase, the first girl is killed, showing some remorse just before she dies, while the leader of the gang is captured, with the film ending with a shot of him on his knees crying, knowing that what awaits him is most probably the electric chair.

What is initially interesting about *Teen-Age Crime Wave* is that although it is exploiting *Blackboard Jungle* (with the film's poster proclaiming unashamedly in large letters that it came 'out of the sidewalk jungle') and was released in November 1955, when the success of rock 'n' roll was in full swing, it has no rock 'n' roll music in its soundtrack. In Chapter 2, when we discuss the genesis of *Rock around the Clock*, we speculate why this may have been the case. For the purposes of this chapter, however, the absence of rock 'n' roll does little to stop audiences from understanding the protagonists as 'teenagers'. Their attire is markedly different from all adults who appear in the film; their use of language, although not teen slang, is confident and befitting their age; their disdain for adult institutions is articulated in any opportunity. Perhaps more importantly, the film includes a subplot about the generation gap and the relationship between parents and children, with the father of the second, innocent, girl willing to let her slip through the juvenile reformation system, an act that he regrets later in the film. In doing this, *Teen-Age Crime Wave* makes a bold statement about failing parents, which will be taken much further by *Rebel without A Cause*. Taking all this into consideration, while the end finds all delinquents dead or captured, redeemed or scared, the closure provided is not particularly reassuring, especially as for 70 out of the 75 minutes of the film's duration, the main teen characters enjoyed fully their delinquent lives.

Running Wild, on the other hand, is not concerned directly with teenagers as the story revolves around a rookie cop infiltrating a ring of car thieves based in a small-town garage. It has no intertitles and no moralistic messages about the generation gap. However, a lot of the early action in the film takes place at the Cove, a shady bar at the outskirts of the town that is portrayed as a den of subcultural activity for young adults. Pinball machines, jukeboxes, swing dancing, strong use of slang, young men with switchblade knives, young girls smoking, drinking and dancing, all contribute to a representation that is conversant with the discourses of misguided youth that dominated the nation at that moment in time. And while swing and jitterbug dancing seem initially out of place, just a few seconds of screen time after the viewers' introduction to the Cove takes place, a young woman (played by Mamie Van Doren) requests 'that Haley's Comets "Razzle Dazzle"' [*sic*], which is immediately selected by a young man in the bar's jukebox.

Stylistically, the film makes the most out of this scene. Van Doren tilts her head suggestively backwards to ask for 'Razzle Dazzle', as the camera stops surveying the bar and frames her in a medium close-up (see Figure 1.3). Together with the fact that she requests the song by mentioning both the title and the band, it is clear that the scene is bracketed from the rest of the film, which has no other references to rock 'n' roll. Furthermore, as soon as the song starts playing the young

Figure 1.3. In a suggestive pose, young Mamie Van Doren asks for 'Razzle Dazzle' in *Running Wild*

patrons move to dance in a far more energetic version of jitterbug than the previous scene. The focus is on Van Doren, who dances with Lou Southern (a dancer who also has a small but important role in *Rock around the Clock*), though in several instances the camera picks her dancing on her own. The editing is considerably faster compared to the other scenes, while as the song ends Van Doren lies ecstatic on a table and tilts back her head again, self-reflexively marking the end of this unusual sequence (see Figure 1.4). Reviews of the film did not miss on the scene's importance, with *Variety* referring to the film's 'use of rock-'n'-roll type of musical background to further emphasise juve appeal' (Brog 1955: 6), and with the *Hollywood Reporter* calling the scene the film's 'high point' in which 'skilled direction really succeeds in animating Mamie Van Doren' (Moffitt 1955: 3). Also released in November 1955, *Running Wild* seems to have been an even stronger example of a film that gave juvenile delinquency a new imaginary (and a new image) thanks to rock 'n' roll than *Blackboard Jungle*. And despite the fact that the film was not about teenagers, its advertising made it explicitly about them by featuring a large picture of Van Doren dancing under the tagline, 'Teen-Age ... Tough and Tempted'.

Given this trajectory of youth-focused American cinema it may come as a surprise that the most famous film representing teenagers in

Figure 1.4. An ecstatic Mamie Van Doren lies on a bar table following her dance to 'Razzle Dazzle'

the mid-1950s, *Rebel without a Cause*, steered clear of rock 'n' roll, even though it placed youth subcultural activities and juvenile delinquency at the centre of its narrative. With the film announced in the trades in December 1954 ('Nick Ray Eastbound' 1954: 2), just as rock 'n' roll music was crossing over to the mainstream and with the shoot starting on 28 March 1955 ('"Rebel without a Cause" ...' 1955: 3), just two weeks after the triumphant release of *Blackboard Jungle*, one wonders why the filmmakers avoided the use of rock 'n' roll. The answer perhaps lies in the fact that it was a relatively big-budget production, shot in Technicolor and CinemaScope, that may not have been able to 'carry' rock 'n' roll as easily as the earlier *Blackboard Jungle* or its contemporaneous *Running Wild*, both shot in black and white. Furthermore, the film's focus on middle class dysfunctional families and the ways in which bad parenting can contribute to teen angst was far removed from multicultural inner-city schools and shady bars patroned by working-class youth where rock 'n' roll seemed to fit more naturally. Instead, the most defining youth-focused film of the 1950s is scored by classical music, while the songs heard from protagonist Jim Stark's car radio come from the 1930s.

Even without the presence of rock 'n' roll, however, *Rebel without a Cause* manages to contribute decidedly to the reimagining of the teenager mid-decade. The story could have been plot driven, exploiting in earnest the spectacle of dangerous youth and juvenile delinquency, as it revolves around the efforts of high school boy Jim Stark (James Dean) to 'fit in' as he struggles in his relationship with a domineering mother (Ann Doran), an emasculated father (Jim Backus), a girlfriend (Natalie Wood) that has her own problems with her parents, a friend (Sal Mineo) that has been abandoned by his own parents and is being bullied, and a school gang led by Buzz (Corey Allen) with whom Jim engages in a deadly car race. Given its production in widescreen and colour, it could have provided strong representations of youth subcultural activities, which no doubt would captivate the young audiences of the film in ways that earlier black and white productions could have not achieved.

However, *Rebel without a Cause* does not adopt this approach. Instead, all these spectacular elements are filtered in the strongest possible way through character psychology, with James Dean's groundbreaking performance becoming the spectacle that dominates the film's style, therefore absorbing all the other spectacular elements. Whether it is the celebrated opening scene of the film where he lies on the street playing with a toy monkey, the scene where he uses a bottle of milk to cool his temper, or the scene where he lies on the sofa with his head hanging backwards off the edge and the camera turns 180 degrees to

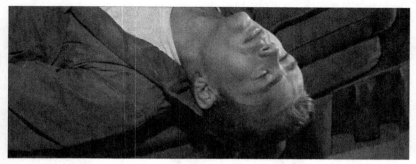

Figure 1.5. James Dean's 'spectacular' performance overwhelms the spectacle of youth subcultural activities in *Rebel without a Cause*

capture his mental state (see Figure 1.5), Jim's psychology as manifested through gesture, expression and body movement dominates the narrative. In this respect, excessive, spectacular and melodramatic moments still exist and provide meaning and pleasure for film viewers (Jim's famous red jacket; Judy's exuberance at the 'chickie race') but they are dominated by Dean's spectacular performance. This allows the film to remain grounded in a classical narrative led by the main character's psychological motivation, while also providing a new kind of representation of youth that chimes with the mid-1950s reimagination of the teenager, despite the complete absence of rock 'n' roll.

From Juvenile Delinquency to Cultural Rebellion

Despite their many differences, what brings together the films above is the connection between subculture and delinquency. Even in *The Wild One* and *Running Wild* where the main characters are clearly adults, this connection between subcultural activities (including rock 'n' roll in the latter example) and crime becomes – seemingly – the only way to define and understand particular groups whose cultural practices differ from the dominant culture. For this reason, when the teenpic emerged in earnest in the second half of the 1950s, the image of the teenage delinquent captured the national imaginary, despite the strong presence of many 'clean' teenpics (Doherty 1988: 188). Inevitably, 'juvenile delinquency' became an overdetermined label, virtually synonymous with all kinds of youth subcultural activities, especially when they took place under the shade of, or in close proximity to, rock 'n' roll.

Such a tendency, however, obscured other possible identities for young people engaging in subcultural activities and is partly responsible for leading scholarly accounts of *Rock around the Clock* to use the term 'juvenile delinquent/cy' to describe that film's representation of youth (see Introduction). One of these identities is that of the 'cultural rebel', which, we argue, is a much more fitting description for the kinds of representation *RATC* advances. To outline its main characteristics and the ways in which it relates to the 'juvenile delinquent' and other youth identities, we turn to the work of Michael Brake and his influential study *Comparative Youth Culture: The Sociology of Youth Culture and Youth Subcultures in America, Britain and Canada* (1985).

Taking his cue from Matza (1962), who argued that youth was a time for rebelliousness and that it manifested often in the form of delinquency, radicalism and bohemianism (Brake 1985: 22), Brake suggested that youth subcultures can be studied within four key traditions: respectable youth, delinquent youth, cultural rebels and politically militant youth (23). Respectable youth are those young people who engage in aspects of teen culture, be it through music, magazines, TV or cinema but who are by and large conforming to dominant cultural ideals, at least to the extent in which any opposition to normative structures is expressed in ways that are 'non-delinquent'. Delinquent youth, like the boys represented in Whyte's 'Street Corner Society', are most commonly teenage boys from working- or lower-class backgrounds. Their leisure time tends to be spent engaging in illegal activities such as 'theft or violence or vandalism', while girls in that group tend to be identified through engagement in 'sexual misbehaviour' (ibid.). Brake strongly emphasises that this group's delinquency is underlined by illegality even if the activities they take part in are commonplace and constitute a way of life within their communities. He also states that the majority of empirical studies of youth focus on this tradition, which may explain its overwhelming presence in accounts of youth film and teenpics.

Brake's third category of youth subcultures, the cultural rebels, is most likely to consist of teenagers from middle-class backgrounds. Well-educated and with access to artistic-literary traditions, these young people tend to occupy the fringes of bohemian cultures rather than being immersed in them (Brake 1985: 23). With bohemianism being identified as 'indifferent to property' and more interested in 'attack[ing] puritanistic and mechanized bureaucratic society' (86), it is clear that cultural rebels are subcultural groups that are not politically threatening or dangerous, especially compared to the fourth youth subcultural category, politically militant youth, which tends to embrace radical politics from 'environmental and community politics to direct militant action' (23). Cultural rebels have the potential to rejuvenate society by helping introduce new mores and attitudes and by challenging a popular culture that has become staid and stale due to extreme levels of standardisation that could be the product of mechanised and bureaucratic practices and which serve the ideology of dominant culture. Furthermore, the middle-class background of the cultural rebels often allows them to experience a fusion between work and leisure – 'work and play' – (84) that is not open to subcultures with lower-class membership as the latter have to maintain this distinction, with work providing them with the means for leisure and play. As we will demonstrate in the final section of this chapter, this fusion represents a significant thematic trait in *RATC*.

Brake's main example of cultural rebellion as a key trait of a youth subculture is the Beat generation, which, although predates rock 'n' roll in terms of genesis (the late 1940s), it reached its peak around the same time as rock 'n' roll with the publication of Allen Ginsberg's *Howl* (1956) and Jack Kerouac's *On the Road* (1957). With its roots harking in post-war France and existentialism, the Beat generation emerged in the US as an individualism-focused, anti-Establishment movement that nonetheless did not seek to instil a new order (Brake 1985: 88). Espousing a life bereft of commitment and in constant search of new visions, members of this subculture experimented with sex and drugs, while part of their disengagement with mainstream American society involved crossing race lines and engaging with cultures that originated from different racial and ethnic groups. As we demonstrate below, *Rock around the Clock* represents rock 'n' roll and the youth involved in it as a subculture characterised by a watered-down form of cultural rebellion, which, not surprisingly, can be co-opted by and integrated in dominant culture.

Youth Subculture, Cultural Rebellion and *Rock around the Clock*

Rock around the Clock opens far away from the world of teenagers and young adults, in an anonymous night club where a big band plays an orchestral version of Harold Arlen and Ted Koehler's 'Let's Fall in Love' (1933). The song is an 'American standard', part of the 'Great American Songbook' that also contains popular and jazz music and songs by such influential composers as Irving Berlin, Cole Porter, the Gershwin brothers and, indeed, Arlen and Koehler, who also composed 'Stormy Weather' together. The dance floor at the night club, however, is almost empty, while the band leader's facial expression clearly suggests that he is annoyed about the situation. As the song ends and the band takes a break, their manager, Steve Hollis, comes in with the news that their residency at the club has been cancelled, for the third time in this tour. He explains that big band music is dead and that people are no longer interested in dancing but, instead, going for new sounds, 'small groups, vocalists, novelty combos'. The band leader disagrees and fires Steve, who is relieved not to be associated any more with such an outdated mode of entertainment. As he jokes, 'maybe I should book you into a schoolhouse during a fire drill, you might be able to clear them fast with the kind of music you are playing'.

The joke is done in a throwaway fashion, but it clearly sets up big band music (and the music cultures it is associated with) not only as staid, stale and antiquated but also as a music that is hated by school children and, by extension, teenagers. Big band music had emerged in the 1920s from smaller 'rough and ready' 'combos of early jazz' (Gioia 1998: 95). Consisting of saxophone, trumpet, trombone and rhythm sections big bands became associated with new forms of vernacular dancing that were introduced on the East Coast, including ones coming from African American traditions (96). Over the course of the next two decades, big band music would continue to evolve, drawing influences from numerous directions, including Tin Pan Alley (which is associated with the Great American Songbook) (ibid.) but also new forms of jazz as these were emerging in Harlem, Chicago and other jazz music hubs. But it was its links with dancing that would bring big band music to its peak in the late 1930s and early 1940s, which is also known as the swing era. Incorporating innovations by Black jazz musicians and focusing its energies on an entertainment hungry public coming out of the Great Depression, swing music dominated the American mainstream until after WW2. Then, Gioia argues, 'a growing economy and rising wages helped kill the big band', which in the context of this new era it resembled 'a bloated relic of a less expensive age' (120).

Gioia's characterisation of big band music as 'a bloated relic' fits well with the established music culture in the *Rock around the Clock* narrative, especially when juxtaposed with the idea of small groups and novelty combos that are necessarily understood as subcultural expressions. At that point the narrative does not provide any more information about the kind of music they are associated with, except for the fact that it is not dance music. In this respect, it is a surprising turn of events when on the way back to New York, Steve and Corny (Henry Slate) (a band member who resigned from the band to join Steve) stop in a small town and see everyone heading to a Saturday night dance. Attributing this to the parochialism of small-town America where the news that no one dances anymore has not arrived yet, they decide nonetheless to check out the town's music scene and see why people are still dancing. This is the next time that 'youth' becomes a point of reference in the film, both visually and aurally. Youngsters spilling out of a T-bird are beeping the horn as Steve's car is blocking the road and calling him a 'daddy-o' (see Figure 1.6), while as soon as Steve and Corny arrive at their motel they are told that the dance is specifically for the 'younglings', which clearly marks them as a dance subculture. This is confirmed emphatically when Steve and Corny approach the dance venue and listen to a type of music they do not recognise.

The emphasis on cultural rebellion comes immediately in sharp focus in this scene. Whatever this music is, it is not something completely new. As Steve and Corny profess, it seems to be a combination of boogie, swing and jive or, in other words, a subculture that has drawn on mainstream music culture to create new music and dance forms that are still connected to existing traditions. Furthermore, the energetic dancing that takes place is clearly based on jitterbug, with a stronger emphasis on acrobatics to draw attention to the fact that it requires a slightly different skillset than swing dancing. Indeed, when Steve (and the audience) first hear what this music (and dance) are called, it is an ecstatic female dancer lying on her dancing partner's back with her head upside down that proclaims: 'it's rock 'n' roll, brother, and we are rockin' tonight' (see Figure 1.7). Unlike the assumptions Steve made about the people of this small town, they have sufficient access to artistic traditions in order to create, if not something radically new (and therefore dangerous or disruptive), something

Figure 1.6. Youngsters spilling out of a T-bird and beeping the horn as Steve's car is blocking the road is the first visual reference to youth cultures in *Rock around the Clock*

Figure 1.7. Cultural rebels update jitterbugging for a new era

that draws on the mainstream and therefore has the potential to rejuvenate it.

This is also clearly confirmed by the fact that the adults of the town
have no issue with either the music or the dancing. The motel owner is
already fluent in rock 'n' roll slang when he sends Steve and Corny to
the dance, making the self-consciously uttered comment 'man, them
two cats don't dig the most at all', while no one seems to be bothered
by the proximity of bodies on the dance floor and the sexual energy
that is created by that. If anything, it looks like that this town is outside any historical reality when such music was seen as an instrument
of corruption and as encouraging the expression of juvenile delinquency. It is also a town that has no African American people and
therefore there is no danger for the new subculture to cross race lines.

A second key manifestation of the cultural rebel subculture comes a
couple of scenes later when Steve tries to convince the town band, Bill
Haley and His Comets, to sign with him so that he can manage them
professionally. Retaining the real name of the band but playing a fictional version of themselves, Haley and his band members appear as
amateur musicians who have working-class jobs (tractor mechanics,
farmhands, seed sellers). However, Steve's negotiations about a deal do
not take place with the clearly adult Haley. Instead, they are conducted
with Lisa Johns, a dancer attached to the band, who is in her early
twenties and therefore represents 'youth' in this part of the action. The
daughter of the motel owner, Lisa is far removed from any working-
class representations. The narrative reveals nothing about her

education background but it is clear that she conducts herself in a middle-class manner. She is well-spoken, without traces of an accent (as compared to Haley), reads *Variety* and is very adept in negotiating with a seasoned manager like Steve an arrangement that is good for the band.

Lisa's surprising middle-class makeup amid a clearly working-class environment cleverly helps with the identification of rock 'n' roll as a non-threatening activity that is firmly situated in cultural rebellion, with very little space for juvenile delinquency (as a later scene will demonstrate) and no space for radical politics. Rock 'n' roll is a new, youth-led subculture that enables today's young people to do what their predecessors did but in their own way. Mainstream music must be rendered antiquated but the new music form connects with it, even if it is presented by Haley as played 'upside down'. As for its raw power and its encouragement of sexual activities, nothing of such nature is in sight under the roof of the town hall where the Saturday dance takes place. And if this institutional vigilance is not sufficient to reassure viewers, the fact that the main dancing couple that demonstrates how rock 'n' roll dancing should take place, consists of a brother and a sister (Lisa and her brother Jimmy, played by Earl Barton) closes down any suspicion of sexual activities being part of this subculture.

To complete the middle-class character of the music, the dance and the subculture, and before agreeing on the split of the profits with Lisa, Steve needs to remove the marks of working-class identity from Bill Haley and His Comets. He does that by convincing the band that what they would do as professionals is not work, but rather a 'fusion between work and play', to use Brake's phrase. Surprised to hear that Haley and the band are paid in onions and turnips for the work they do on Saturdays and that they have blue collar jobs for the rest of the week to be able to afford gigs in which they are paid in kind, Steve is very clear in his pitch of the band 'fusing' work and play: 'what if every night was Saturday night'? In presenting playing music as not work that is nonetheless handsomely remunerated, Steve introduces Haley to certain middle-class conceptions about 'work' that include careers in arts and entertainment that are not easily open to working-class youth. Finally, Steve completes the transformation of the working-class Bill Haley and His Comets to a middle class-band by calling the band leader 'Mr Haley'. Surprised by the title, Haley questions its use before Steve explains his vision for the band's success from coast to coast. From that point and until the end of the film, Haley and his band will be wearing strictly formal clothes that enhance their image as a middle-class outfit. The semi-formal jacket and shirt in their first performance give way to tuxedos and other formal wear in later scenes when they play in public, with only rehearsal scenes portraying the band members in informal checked shirts.

Given the level of this makeover, it is not surprising that this middle-class dressed youth music and dance subculture has a relatively easy job to be accepted nationally. The big test takes place in an exclusive girls' school prom in Hartford, CT. The talent agency had booked the band there with a view to ridiculing them, not because it had an issue with the music and dance, but because agency owner Corinne Talbot (Alix Talton) wanted to shut down Steve's budding romance with Lisa. Scheduled to follow Tony Martinez and His Band who play a watered-down version of a Latino-inspired music for the upper-class teenagers, rock 'n' roll is expected to be such a contrast that would scandalise the young dancers and end the band's (and Steve's career). Dressed in immaculate tuxedos Bill Haley and His Comets start playing 'Razzle Dazzle', but no one is getting up to dance. Lisa and her brother break the ice and start dancing, strictly avoiding any jitterbug acrobatics and using a routine that would not be too far removed from an Astaire and Rogers musical (see Figure 1.8). A few seconds later, and after a couple of shots showing the teens 'getting the beat', the dance floor is filled with young couples, who accept the music and its dance as respectable forms of entertainment. Compare this with *Running Wild*, and the working-class youth in the Cove bar, led by Mamie Van Doren's wildly sexualised dance and the car-stealing delinquents that provide the narrative action to that film.

Figure 1.8. A very different, non-sexualised form of dancing to 'Razzle Dazzle', compared to that in *Running Wild*

Still, on one occasion, *Rock around the Clock* entertains the possibility of juvenile delinquency and rejection by the older generation, only for both to be dismissed immediately as unacceptable positions. After the first few notes of 'Razzle Dazzle', the camera cuts to the teachers' table, consisting of one male and two female middle-aged chaperones who look towards the stage in disbelief. A few seconds later, the film returns to the same shot showing each of the two female teachers proclaiming the spectacle in front of their eyes 'infamous' and 'barbaric'. Another few seconds later and one of the women gets up and asks the male teacher to 'stop them' and 'do something'. But before he registers his response, a young dancing couple stops in front of their table and the teenage girl threatens to stop her father's donation of a new library to the school. Her behaviour shocks the teacher who walks away as the young couple continues to dance. But if this behaviour is coded as deviant or even delinquent, it is immediately dismissed as the scene moves to the remaining two teachers and shows the male asking the female one to dance. The latter is also shocked by the invitation and walks away leaving the male teacher alone but visibly content to see the young people having a good time. As for the young female student who misbehaved, there are no repercussions. After all, if the dance had been stopped, the school would have missed on a major new educational asset.

The two female teachers' rejection of rock 'n' roll is conversant with the subculture's cultural rebel identity. As Brake argues, cultural rebels are interested in attacking 'puritanistic' aspects of society, which the conservative styled teachers certainly represent. Indeed, this (barely registered) rejection of rock 'n' roll by the puritan middle-aged teachers gives the subculture credibility – after all, if there was no resistance at any point in its trajectory, this would never be a subculture. Similarly, rock 'n' roll's rejection by the owner of the talent agency is only partly motivated by the subculture's potential for deviancy and is also easily rebuffed. As mentioned above, the female owner of the talent agency booked Bill Haley and His Comets to an exclusive girls' school prom, expecting that it would not be appropriate for the environment, because she wanted to kill off Steve's romance with Lisa. Failing on both accounts, she brings up the subcultural card by saying to Lisa, 'Excellent! You succeeded in making a bunch of whirling dervishes girls who were brought up to be ladies.' The 20-year-old Lisa, however, does not take the bait and returns the conversation to business with the ironic 'I am sorry we pleased the audience, Ms Talbot. I thought that's what we were supposed to do.'

With cultural rebellion also aiming its arrows at mechanised bureaucracy, Lisa's statement can be read as a comment on the subculture's potential to rejuvenate popular entertainment, which has become staid and antiquated, a bloated relic of an earlier era, the product of a mass production system that is not fit for purpose. This is confirmed a few minutes later, after the performance of 'Teach You to Rock' by the (also) tuxedoed Freddie Bell and the Bellboys. Steve offers a full bill to the agency, with Bill Haley and His Comets, 'the kids' (Lisa and her brother) and Freddie Bell and the Bellboys only to get the response that 'these sorts of acts are not in our line'. That 'line' will be swiftly challenged. As soon as Alan Freed helps Steve by featuring his artists in New York's West River Club, the talent agency becomes inundated by requests for rock 'n' roll bookings. There is no doubt that eventually a new mechanised bureaucracy will be introduced so that rock 'n' roll is integrated in the mainstream and that this middle-class-dressed, cultural rebel-led subculture will become popular culture. For the time, though, it is presented as something new and exciting.

Conclusion

This chapter examined the representation of young people *in Rock around the Clock* through the prism of subcultures and in particular the category of the 'cultural rebel' (rather than the juvenile delinquent), which the film conceives as being at the vanguard of new sounds, new dance styles and new ways of linguistic expression. As we argued, the film somewhat undermines the cultural rebels' subcultural capital by allowing these characters to operate at the intersection of classes (rural, working class but educated sufficiently to understand how deals and business contracts work), gender (Lisa is a dancer but also the manager of the band) and even generations (Lisa's father is well-versed in the subculture's linguistic slang and provides no opposition to his daughter involvement in rock 'n' roll). However, it is clear that this flexibility and elasticity are essential to turn this new subculture, which originates in the (geographical) margins, into a popular culture that will operate nationally. Furthermore, such a move also undermines the subculture's cachet and signals its instant commodification and recuperation, arguably best exemplified in the idea that the fictional Bill Haley and His Comets will stop being paid in onions and turnips and start get paid in real money.

On the other hand, the film's conceptualisation of the cultural rebel does not preclude its recuperation by the system. Borrowing more from bohemianism rather than delinquency and radicalism (Brake 1985: 86) and privileging more an attack on the mechanised bureaucratic society (as this is represented by Corinne Talbot's leading national booking agency) than the puritanical society of the time (which is only marginally represented by two female teachers), the film presents the cultural rebels clustered around rock 'n' roll music as nothing short of a breath of fresh air that would be good to sweep the rest of the county. Blowing from the countryside to the big urban centres and the rest of the nation, it breathes new life to a seemingly moribund music business and night life, while its carefully managed dissemination to the nation's youth ensures that any potentially threatening elements – that may or may not come from its (non-existent in the film) links to delinquency or radicalism – will be ironed out. What starts as cultural rebellion is smoothly repackaged as cultural conformity, which is Brake's first subcultural youth category.

2   Who's Exploiting What and How (1)

Rock around the Clock and Exploitation Formulas in an Industry in Transition

In many ways the production and release of *Rock around the Clock* reflects the process that the film's narrative dramatises: a producer, with a keen eye on following trends in film and other cultural industries, puts together a carefully packaged and managed film to cash in on a youth subcultural activity (listening and dancing to rock 'n' roll music) that was becoming increasingly visible at the time. Or, to put it differently, the narrative and style of the film are determined by the very specific production and distribution contexts in the margins of the American film industry, which encouraged the making of particular types of films that could appeal to youth demographics. These margins were being realigned in the 1950s as conditions in the film industry at large had been changing due to the confluence of factors that, as Tino Balio suggested, included: 'increased competition, a dwindling audience, constricting foreign markets, television, and the consequences of the *Paramount* decision' (Balio 1976: 202).

In this new environment, what was previously (in the 1930s and 1940s) designated as B-unit film production for the major Hollywood studios, and low-end independent film production for an array of smaller companies, started to evolve. This evolution was gradual and its origins can be traced back in the late 1940s, when the changing conditions in the American film industry coincided with sweeping social changes and developments in the country (suburbanisation and new leisure opportunities, the impact of the Cold War and an increasing political repression, among others) that also signalled the changing function of cinema as a cultural practice. The outcome of this evolution, however, became clearer in the mid-1950s when the teen demographic had made its presence strongly felt and this kind of production started increasingly to coalesce around the principle of making films that targeted primarily that particular audience.

The rest of the chapter will provide a summary of the factors that contributed to this new environment for low-budget filmmaking that

DOI: 10.4324/9781315544908-3

became intricately linked to what became known as exploitation film practices, before turning its attention to Sam Katzman. Often referred to as the 'king of exploitation cinema' (quoted in Baker 2013: 94), Katzman, whose career goes all the way back to the early years of B-unit and low-end independent production in the 1930s, arguably exemplifies best this development in American cinema of the 1950s, before filmmakers like Roger Corman, Russ Meyer and others took it to other directions in the 1960s and beyond. After discussing Katzman's filmmaking practices and the extent to which they shaped and were shaped by the emerging exploitation film models of the time through a brief examination of a cycle of films about corrupt city officials in the years just prior to starting making teenpics, the chapter will embark on a detailed analysis of *RATC* as an exploitation film production. It will focus on the ways in which Katzman 'exploited' the song 'Rock around the Clock' as the origin for the film and as the cornerstone for the distribution approach he developed together with Columbia executives.

From B Film to Exploitation: A Portrait of an Industry in Turmoil

By the late 1920s the American film industry had settled in its classic oligopolistic structure that was dominated by the so-called 'Big Five' studios (Paramount, MGM, Warner Bros., Fox Film Corporation and RKO) and the 'Little Three' (Universal, Columbia and United Artists). These companies were able to control the industry through organising themselves in a vertical structure whereby all three aspects of the supply chain (production, distribution and exhibition) were under their direct ownership and management.[1] According to Douglas Gomery, during the studio era (late 1920s to late 1940s), these eight companies were responsible for the production of three quarters of all US films released annually, while the theatres they operated directly or through affiliations with independent exhibitors were often generating as much as 90% of all revenues (Gomery 1986: 9).

The rest of the production was handled by a wide array of independent companies that ranged from small, well organised studios such as Monogram and Republic that were producing dozens of low-budget productions annually to opportunistic outfits that often made and released a handful of films before being squeezed out of the market. Scrapping for the remaining 10% of exhibition revenues, it was clear that they were not in a position to dedicate large budgets to their films or to take risks with their product. As a result, they specialised in an efficient, no-frills production from which they were all but guaranteed a small profit for their films. This was because their films tended to be sold to independent exhibitors for a flat fee (rather than a percentage of the box-office revenues that was the model for major studio productions) that was not determined by attendance and popularity (Flynn and McCarthy 1975: 17). For this reason, knowing the number of theatres that would buy their films and the fee that each exhibitor would pay meant that independent producers could budget accordingly in order to record a profit.

The reason why these low-end independent film companies operated with this level of certainty was because the Great Depression that followed the Wall Street crash of 1929 and lasted until the US involvement in WW2 had created demand for a number of films that could not be met by the studios alone. As John Izod explains, the Depression prompted exhibitors as early as 1930 to initiate the practice of the double bill whereby two features together with other short subjects would create an approximately 3-hour programme that was deemed good value for money (Izod 1988: 98). The success of this scheme changed the structure of the industry and gave birth to what became known as the B film (taking its name from its lower position on the bill). With major studio productions and top-rank independent films by a small cadre of established producers designated as the A films, the B films were immediately understood as utilitarian productions, the role of which was to complete the double bill. With the A film guaranteeing exhibition to the B film, it is not surprising that the latter were sold on a flat fee basis as attendance and popularity were important only for the former.

This development is directly responsible for the establishment of a number of low-end independent film companies in the 1930s. However, what complicates matters was that the major studios were also heavily involved in the production of B films, which suggests that this kind of production did not only operate in the margins of the industry. Indeed, as Balio has argued, without the B films, 'the studio system would have rested on shaky ground'. This is because as a group B films 'collected enough [...] to lower studio overhead, which enabled the majors to operate year round at full capacity' (Balio 1995: 12). With even the most prominent studios such as MGM and Paramount not having the resources to produce 40 or 50 films a year with major stars and impressive production values, it is clear that the B film allowed the industry as a whole to operate in a balanced way that helped it weather the Depression.

But in the 1940s conditions slowly started to change. Although the double bill persisted throughout the decade, the major studios gradually shifted their emphasis on better quality pictures. Partly driven by an improved marketplace during the WW2 build up and partly by a consent decree they signed in 1940 following an anti-trust lawsuit brought by the US government for practising oligopolistic trading methods, the studios started to change strategy (Schatz 1999: 45). Studios such as Warner Bros. ceased B productions completely (Schatz 1996: 300) while 20th Century-Fox subcontracted it to independent producers (Schatz 1999: 335) who nonetheless had a strong relationship with the studios and often used their resources to the extent that they operated more as in-house unit producers. Sam Katzman was one such producer who, after working in a number of low-end independent companies, such as Victory and Monogram, moved to Columbia in 1946 ('Katzman Rolls ...' 1946: 2) and worked as an independent but on a long-term distribution contract with the studio that made him look more like an in-house producer.

These developments initially seemed to benefit the low-end independents who started to have less competition from the studios. However, the former group of companies was not in a position to reap the benefits of this reduced competition. The introduction of television in 1947 provided a new and immediate competitor, especially as a lot of early TV programming, shot cheaply for the requirements of a brand new medium, tended to approximate the low-budget film that was the bread and butter of low-end independents (Davis 1997: 31). Indeed, pretty soon, the old B films were actually transformed into television programmes as such. Realising that this type of programming was successful with the ever expanding television audiences, companies such as Republic and Monogram decided to sell parts of their libraries of films to television as early as 1951 and earn profits at a time when the future of the double bill seemed to be all but foregone ('Republic Okays ...' 1951: 3).

At the same time, while the studios phased out their B film production, it did not mean that they had stopped making low-budget films altogether. Although the majority of their resources as US-based financers-producers went to a small number of films with strong commercial potential, as global distributors they had to continue to trade in volume in order to cover their operation costs around the world. However, what changed was the utility of these low-budget productions, which were increasingly required to work as *standalone* releases and *not* as the second feature in a double bill. This impacted the overall approach to producing these films as well as to marketing them for release.

With the budget of these productions not drastically improving and with their aesthetic quality remaining (often decidedly) inferior compared to the major film releases by the Hollywood studios, it was a very specific set of elements that signalled American film industry's move from B to exploitation film. On the level of production, one of the key elements was the choice of subject matter that could distinguish the film in a marketplace where normally only major studio releases could afford distinction as they tended to be based on pre-sold properties such as Broadway spectacles, best-selling novels or plays. Such subject matter could be a timely topic that was in the news and therefore debated in public discourse, a taboo subject that could offer thrills and titillation but which was avoided by major productions in fear of offending part of their audience or, indeed, a cultural trend, fashion or fad that enjoyed visibility and publicity before inevitably fading away.

A second key element was a new style of filmmaking that would help distinguish these films from the B films of the previous decades and from television series. Given this new type of subject matter that they were focusing on, it is not surprising that (some of) the exploitation films often utilised a style of filmmaking that, for Blair Davis, was 'decidedly rawer and inherently more risky' than the style of most of the B films of the 1930s and 1940s (Davis 2012: 10). For instance, a lot of the crime dramas that thrived in the early 1950s made extensive use of location shooting that provided them with an immediacy, and even a documentary feel, that separated them from studio-bound TV dramas and B films. No longer tied to the low part of a double bill, these films could dare to innovate and reap the benefits if successful at the box office.

Finally, in order to be able to function as standalone releases, low-budget films in the 1950s also needed to have a longer duration than a lot of the B films of the 1930s and 1940s that were often close to the 60-minute mark and sometimes less than that. Indeed, the minimum duration shifted to closer to 75 minutes, with *Rock around the Clock* being 77 minutes long, and most of Sam Katzman-produced films also being around that mark. Once again, such duration also differentiated them further from television programming, including some of these companies' earlier films, which, following their sale for television broadcasting, were edited down to 48 minutes in order to fit to one-hour slots complete with commercials.

It is in the realm of distribution, however, that these low-budget films from both studios and independent companies saw a big transformation. Prior to the 1950s, exploitation films tended to be made completely outside the film industry (Osgerby 2003: 102). Not regulated by industry associations and exhibited primarily through four-wall arrangements whereby producers would rent independent theatres outright or screen films in makeshift exhibition spaces (Chute 1986: 33), exploitation film became intricately linked with the taboo and the forbidden: miscegenation, abortion, venereal diseases, childbirth and drug use, and others (35). The nature of the films' subject matter and their exhibition outside the commercial theatre circuit, often as part of fairs and other amusement attractions, necessitated publicity strategies that relied on showmanship. As one producer put it, audiences 'don't come to see a picture, they come to see a show' (Ripps, quoted in Chute 1986: 39). In this respect, showmanship, based on highly imaginative, ingenious and, more often than not, outlandish methods of publicity, became the cornerstone of distribution practices for producers and distributors of such films.

Exploitation and showmanship quickly found their way into the arsenal of cheap publicity methods for the producers and distributors of B films in the 1940s. However, the 1950s and the conditions of the industry described previously made exploitation filmmaking a more industry-widespread and -integrated strategy. American Releasing Corporation, a new low-budget independent company established in 1954 and specialising in old style B films, quickly shifted its emphasis to exploitation film, rebranded as American International Pictures and adopted the slogan 'Dedicated to Showmanship' (Staehling 1975: 114). Equally, older production and distribution companies were increasingly embracing the exploitation film model, often rebranding in order to stop being associated with the B film as was the case with Monogram, which in 1953 changed its name to Allied Artists.

It was at this point that the exploitation film approach started to shift towards the teenpic, with Doherty suggesting that the courtship between these companies and the teen audience started in 'earnest' in 1955 (Doherty 1988: 3). However, teenagers did not only give exploitation film companies an audience. As we discussed in the previous chapter, they gave them a subject matter that was topical and timely, as their lives, their habits, their culture started to be paraded relentlessly across the US media and cultural institutions. Even more importantly, they gave them a subject matter that could be represented (exploited) in a number of ways, ranging from the licentiousness of juvenile delinquency and teen crime to the horror of growing up, reframed as countless monster and sci fi stories, to the wholesomeness of the 'clean teenpics' that aimed to appease the older generations, while at the same time trying to sell a commercially-friendly culture to its target audience (Doherty 1988: 115, 142, 198, 221). Whatever the angle, confrontational or reassuring, the distribution organisations handling these films were guaranteed to play up sensationalist elements, in the process adapting exploitation techniques to the needs of an industry in transition and adopting them in a widespread fashion. Rock 'n' roll films complete this range of exploitation teenpics of the 1950s in Doherty's account. With rock 'n' roll music hitting the mainstream in 1955 and linked inextricably with youth cultures and subcultures, it was a matter of time for it to become fodder for film exploitation. As we already noted in Chapter 1, *Rock around the Clock* represented teenagers and young people by exploiting rock 'n' roll's status as cultural rebellion, while completely removing aspects of the rock 'n' roll subculture that could be considered more threatening. Other films that followed continued to exploit rock 'n' roll (and used some of the elements that made *RATC* a box-office success) but overall adopted different approaches and strategies within the exploitation spectrum. The next section will examine Sam Katzman's perspective on exploitation film in the 1950s, before providing an account of the film's production and distribution.

Sam Katzman and the Business of Exploitation

In a career spanning five decades, from the early 1930s to the early 1970s, and with approximately 240 credits as a producer,[2] Sam Katzman made 105 of these pictures in the 1950s. In the words of Richard Thompson, Katzman was 'one of the cultural technicians that made the 1950s what they were' (Thompson 1975: 72). His 1950s pictures consist of 89 features and 16 serials. Perhaps more incredibly, 90 of these 105 titles (including all 16 serials) were produced in the seven-year period 1950–56, an average of 13 productions a year. Before the 1950s, he averaged 7 pictures per year (71 titles in total in the 1940s), while in the 1930s he averaged approximately 6 (41 titles between 1933 and 1939). In the 1960s his pace slowed down considerably, releasing 22 titles in total, while he also produced two films in the early 1970s before his death in 1973 at the age of 72.

As these statistics suggest, Katzman was involved in 1950s filmmaking having already produced over 110 pictures during the B-film era of the 1930s and 1940s. These credits were primarily while he worked for two low-end independent companies, Victory Pictures in the 1930s and Monogram until 1947. The latter hired Katzman as an independent producer who specialised in film series (such as the East Side Kids instalments) and produced his pictures under various corporate names such as Four Bell Productions and Banner Productions ('Independent Activity …' 1939: 24). In 1945, Katzman made a deal with Columbia to produce serials, while still keeping his distribution

contract with Monogram ('Katzman Inks ...' 1945: 3). But after deli-
vering titles to both companies in 1946 he released his last film for
Monogram in January 1947 before he made his contract with Columbia exclusive.

One aspect of Katzman's story that has not received due attention
was the extent to which his move from a low-end independent company to a studio impacted his filmmaking. Although he continued to
make low-budget films at a breakneck speed as an independent con-
tractor, his switch to Columbia provided Katzman with the resources
of a studio that were decidedly superior to the ones he could access at
Monogram. Higher budgets, better trained cast and crew, better
equipped sound stages, distribution contracts worldwide, access to
better theatres in the US – all represented 'classier' arrangements for
Katzman than the ones he was used to before (Hanke 1995: 8).
Columbia, as one of the Little Three, was originally located closer to
the bigger low-end independents such as Republic and Monogram
rather than the Big Five. However, by the late 1940s and early 1950s
it had started to upgrade its product through deals with top-rank
independent producers such as Stanley Kramer and Humphrey
Bogart (Gomery 1986: 11), while in 1953 its production *From Here to
Eternity* (Zinnemann) won eight Academy Awards and was the second
biggest box-office success for the year behind *The Robe* (Koster) (Finler
2003: 358).

One can safely suggest then that Columbia provided Katzman with
the resources he needed to make his shift to exploitation filmmaking
more assertively than if he had stayed with Monogram/Allied Artists.
Columbia's resources may also be responsible for Katzman's increased
film production pace in the 1950s. It was certainly through the studio
that Katzman started to collaborate with directors Fred F. Sears and
William Castle, who, in the six year period between 1953 and 1958
directed 43 (26 and 17, respectively) titles out of a total 61 pictures
Katzman produced. Sears, in particular, who was also the director of
Rock around the Clock, rose through the ranks at Columbia, first as an
actor and then as director in the Durango Kid series, B westerns that
Columbia produced and released throughout the 1940s. According to
Dixon, it was his 'speed and prolificity' that brought him to Katzman's
attention who wanted a reliable director who could work at the same
speed as him (Dixon 2005: 78). Robert E. Kent, one of the two
screenwriters for *RATC* was another Columbia employee who became
a close collaborator with Katzman. Between 1951 and 1962 Kent was
responsible for 27 screenplays for Katzman productions, while adding
five more after 1963 when Katzman started to release his films with

other distributors. As Dixon explains, Kent 'was very reliable. He would do, three, four, five screenplays, and then he would rewrite everybody else's screenplays on top of that. It didn't take Kent long to knock out a screenplay' (51).

Besides these above-the-line collaborators, Katzman also had access to a large number of other practitioners who repeatedly worked in his productions and who were also sourced by the producer at Columbia. Henry Freulich, a long-established cinematographer in Columbia's B films in the 1940s, worked a remarkable 33 times with Katzman between 1952 and 1956, even though Katzman opted for Benjamin H. Kline when it came to shooting *RATC*. The latter was another long-term Columbia employee in the 1930s and 1940s, before he started to work for television in the 1950s. After *RATC*, Kline photographed another 15 Katzman productions in the 1956–58 period. Art director Paul Palmentola designed a staggering 98 of Katzman's 105 productions in the 1950s, with their collaboration going all the way back to 1945. Equally, his sound engineer J.S. Westmoreland worked on most Katzman productions since the late 1940s, including on *RATC*, as did set decorator Sidney Clifford.

As is clear, then, Columbia's studio status enabled Katzman to identify collaborators with substantial experience in efficient production but at a level that was superior to what was available in Poverty Row studios. It is also clear that Katzman's production outfit operated at an industrial level rather than a top-rank, boutique independent one whereby an outfit produces a small number or even one film per year. This explains why Katzman embraced fully (and in the process helped shape) the model of exploitation filmmaking that took off in the 1950s. Not expecting a particular film to make a significant profit he went for volume of production and its limited revenues, which nonetheless could add up given the number of films he produced every year in the 1950s.

In his detailed examination of Katzman's production practices, Doherty pinpoints to *Teen-Age Crime Wave*, Katzman's 1955 production focusing on juvenile delinquent youth on the run, as 'a forewarning of future trends and as preparation for exploiting them' (Doherty 1988: 78). Doherty admits that the film did not have any rock 'n' roll music or references to it and functioned more as a melodrama rather than a teenpic. However, he highlights the marketing strategy behind the film as important because it may have been the first campaign to encourage exhibitors to use rock 'n' roll music in order to attract an audience to the theatres (78–9). *Teen-Age Crime Wave* may enable one to see a forewarning of future trends related to rock 'n' roll in the fields of publicity and distribution. However, Katzman's series of films on the corruption of big US city officials and their links to the mob that were based on true stories (six features from 1954 to 1956) arguably represents a better example to showcase his exploitation film practices. Produced by Katzman, four of these films were directed by Sears and two by Castle. Four were written by Kent. Five were photographed by Freulich, with Kline doing the job for the sixth picture, all shot in black and white. Palmentola and Clifford did the art direction and set decoration, respectively, in all six films of the series, while Westmoreland was responsible for the sound in five of them. As we argue, when it came to rock 'n' roll teenpics Katzman only changed the subject matter and the target audience as he deployed the same team of collaborators and approach to the topic.

The first of these pictures, *The Miami Story* (Sears, 1954), includes many key ingredients to exploitation filmmaking. It opens with a montage sequence that explains how organised crime took over Miami. The sequence incorporates a direct audience address by real-life Senator George Smathers, who validates the film's exposé status, before stating how 'ably' the film shows 'what a few courageous citizens, honest politicians and tough alert police agencies can do to rid their cities of gangland's influence'. The rest of the film dramatises this effort within the context of the crime drama genre, making good use of location shooting. Indeed, Dixon reveals that Katzman was originally planning to shoot the film on the backlot in Los Angeles as the plot for the film was originally based on a police case in that city (Dixon 2005: 91). However, the success of films such as *The Enforcer* (Windust, 1951) and *Hoodlum Empire* (Kane, 1952) that were based on the hearings by the US Senate's Special Committee to Investigate Crime in Interstate Commerce (Hoberman 2014: R11) and the possibility of including testimonies from high-ranked politicians involved in the hearings, which were initially convened in Miami before moving to different cities (R21), convinced Katzman to change the location to South Florida.

Such a change immediately increased the marketability of his film. Now Katzman was able to link the story not just to a local police case but to a pressing issue of national importance; he was able place his film in the same tradition as particular films that were inspired by the same issue such as the major studio releases *The Enforcer, The Captive City* (Wise, 1952), *The Turning Point* (Dieterle, 1952) and Columbia's own *The Big Heat* (Lang, 1953), which, according to Dixon, Sears had seen and had asked Katzman to make a film along these lines (Dixon 2005: 89–91); he was able to utilise particular elements from each of these titles to fit his low-budget version (the inclusion of a real life politician endorsing the film from *The Captive City*; the authentic locations from *The Turning Point* and, again according to Dixon, even a subplot from *The Big Heat*) (89).

However, arguably, Katzman's most inspiring choice was to include the name of a real American city on the title. Previous crime films refused to go that far (according to Peter Lev, John Huston's desire to make the location of his 1950 crime drama *The Asphalt Jungle* specific was met with disapproval by MGM's legal department [Lev 2006: 42]). Localising the narrative and the action, on the other hand, gave *The Miami Story* both a distinctiveness and the possibility of exploiting claims to historical accuracy (especially when the production secured the participation of Senator Smathers who gave his endorsement in the opening sequence). Furthermore, the explicit focus on Miami became a focal point when it came to the film's distribution, with the movie posters highlighting the city's mob connections and including newspaper style text about it. Not wanting to put all his eggs in one basket, Katzman also took the opportunity to link his film to *The Big Heat*, when he included the tagline 'How Miami Put the Big Heat on the Mob'.

Sensing the beginning of a new cycle, Katzman moved swiftly to the production of more similar films, keeping the key ingredients that made *The Miami Story* a success, while adding new elements to avoid repetition by tying the narratives of the films as close to news about big cities as possible. *New Orleans Uncensored* (Castle, 1955) was released in March 1955 and *Chicago Syndicate* (Sears, 1955) four months later in July. *Inside Detroit* (Sears) followed in January 1956, *The Houston Story* (Castle) in February 1956 and *Miami Exposé* (Sears) in September 1956. With the release of *Teen-Age Crime Wave* and *Rock around the Clock* also squeezed in among these films in November 1955 and March 1956, respectively, it is clear that the corrupt city officials film cycle was in full swing when Katzman decided to start new cycles with various types of teenpics. In this respect, picking up another trendy topic (rock 'n' roll), securing the participation of some of its real life stars to play themselves, choosing the title of an existing song as the title of his film to link it both to a presold property and a historical cultural moment, invoking a successful film that had previously used that song (*Blackboard Jungle*) and using the same group of collaborators, represent yet another project for Katzman's incredibly well-oiled exploitation film-making machine.

The Genesis of *Rock around the Clock*

The commercial success of rock 'n' roll music and especially its strong visibility in popular discourse as a morally corrupting force for the nation's youth gave Katzman an obvious subject to exploit. The music had started to become popular with a wider demographic in early 1955, with *Variety* reporting on 19 January that 'the r & b influence has now crossed all color lines into the general pop market' and crediting Alan Freed's radio shows and rock 'n' roll parties in New York as 'the tipping point' (Schoenfeld 1955: 49). Two weeks after *Variety's* article, the *Hollywood Reporter* ran a piece about 'a novel musical score' being approved for MGM's *Blackboard Jungle* that included the song 'Rock around the Clock' by Bill Haley and His Comets ('Note Book' 1955: 7). Around the same time (late winter/early spring of 1955), songs such as 'Honey Love', 'Crying in the Chapel', 'Maybellene', 'Hound Dog', 'Ain't that a Shame' and 'Shake, Rattle and Roll' met with great success by young listeners and dancers, writes Douglas Brode (2015: xxix). But it was the release of *Blackboard Jungle* on 19 March 1955 and its inclusion of 'Rock around the Clock' in the opening and closing credits that became a catalyst for further popularising rock 'n' roll but also for linking it to youth crime and the image of juvenile delinquency.

Only two months after the film's release, in May 1955, 'Rock around the Clock', a record that was originally recorded by Bill Haley and His Comets in April 1954 and released without much success,[3] found itself on the *Billboard* charts. Labelling this 'an interesting comeback', *Billboard* asserted that the record's return on the charts after a long absence was due to the success of *Blackboard Jungle*, which 'spark[ed] a new sales demand for the platter' ('Chart Comments' 1955: 30). On 9 July 1955, the record reached the No 1 spot and stayed there for eight weeks (Stanfield 2015: 105). By the end of the year, it had reportedly sold over 2 million copies in the US alone (Altschuler 2003: 33) and was a top selling record in other markets, especially in the UK ('Haley's "Clock" ...' 1955: 1). At the same time, fuelled by the success of its soundtrack, *Blackboard Jungle* proved to be MGM's top grossing film in 1955, landing on the 12th place of the annual North American box-office charts with rentals of $5.2 million (Arneel 1956: 1).

As we mentioned above, in 1955 Katzman produced 13 films for Columbia in a variety of genres, with *Teen-Age Crime Wave* being the only picture dealing with subject matter related to youth. That film was already in the pipeline in June 1955 ('"Gimmick" Sub ...' 1955: 22), just as 'Rock around the Clock' was dominating the charts. Perhaps unwilling to make changes to the original sound design plans that would increase the film's overall budget, Katzman did not use rock 'n' roll music in that film, missing the opportunity to ride the wave of *Blackboard Jungle*'s notoriety and the associations of rock 'n' roll with juvenile delinquency. On the other hand, by the time that the film was ready for release in late October 1955, Katzman could not have ignored the opportunities afforded by the sweeping success of rock 'n' roll and together with Columbia orchestrated a marketing campaign designed to link the film with that music in order to attract customers to the theatres (Doherty 1988: 78–9).

It is exactly at this point in time that Katzman decided to do *Rock around the Clock*, with the *Hollywood Reporter* announcing the film on 14 November 1955 ('Katzman Musical ...' 1955: 4), just two weeks after the release of *Teen-Age Crime Wave*. With no stars or director confirmed and with the script being written on the basis that it needed to fit the title 'Rock around the Clock', this was looking like the epitome of exploitation film. *Variety* confirmed this two weeks later in an article with the subheading 'Sam Katzman Exploits Music Fad – Columbia to Release' ('A Rock 'n' Roll Feature' 1955: 4). The trade paper also confirmed the participation of Bill Haley and His Comets (ibid.), a major coup for Katzman given the level of success the band was enjoying at that particular moment in time. Finally, in order to be able to use 'Rock around the Clock' as the title of his film, Katzman and Columbia made an agreement with James E. Myers, one of the two co-writers of the song (the other being Max C. Freedman ['Myers Makes ...' 1956: 16]).

Previous scholarly work on the film has outlined in detail Katzman's skills in securing Bill Haley and His Comets and the other bands that appear in *RATC*. The producer was acquainted with Jolly Joyce, owner of the well-established Jolly Joyce Theatrical Agency (Denisoff and Romanowski 1990: 68). Jolly Joyce himself had become the band's manager in the summer of 1954, just a few months after Bill Haley and His Comets switched record labels from Essex to Decca in the spring of the same year ('Haley and Comets ...' 1954: 58). According to Dawson, Joyce also represented Tony Martinez and His Band and Freddie Bell and the Bellboys, and he insisted that Katzman used all three acts in his film as they were offered together as a package with Bill Haley and His Comets (Dawson 2005: 149). Dawson also reports that Haley and his band were paid $20,000 for their appearance (ibid.), though it is not clear if this fee also included the rights to the song's performance in the film and its exploitation in other media.[4]

Having three acts confirmed with Bill Haley and His Comets as the headline, Katzman also secured The Platters. Although as a doo-wop group its relationship to rock 'n' roll was rather tenuous (Gillett 1996: 52), The Platters was the most successful outfit in terms of hit records in the rock 'n' roll era (ibid.). Perhaps more importantly, they were the only Black act in the film and therefore the only connection to the Black heritage of the music and its links to 'race' and rhythm and blues records, which is otherwise completely effaced from the film. As a result, the group's participation in *RATC* helped legitimise the film's attempt to tell, as one of the poster's taglines proclaims, the 'whole story of rock 'n' roll'. Equally importantly, it represented a second major attraction in the film's credits after Bill Haley and His Comets.

The final ingredient was the signing of Alan Freed. By the end of 1955, Freed had become a major player in a number of media indus- tries due to the success of rock 'n' roll and the role he had played in promoting and popularising it. Writing about the increasingly sig- nificant role of the disc jockey, *Billboard* reported how 'extra-curricular activities' had become big business for DJs such as Freed who operated in a number of fields, including writing songs, packaging and hosting stage shows, supervising recordings, having his own band and doing concerts and records with it (Bundy 1955: 11). To this list of activities Freed added acting and being a 'technical advisor' in a major motion picture (ibid.), which, given the nature of the topic of the film, would also generate further business deals for him. Indeed, the film's release in March 1956 coincided with the scheduling of a number of rock 'n' roll shows hosted by Freed (Denisoff and Romanowski 1990: 73), which, no doubt, cross-promoted each other and helped increase both the com- mercial success and notoriety of *RATC*. Like Bill Haley and His Comets, Freed was paid $20,000 for his services (Dawson 2005: 146).

With the main attractions of the film in place, Katzman cast the rest of the (acting) parts with actors with long tenures in the B film and television sectors. Johnny Johnston, Alix Talton, Lisa Gaye, Earl Barton and John Archer (Mike Dodd) (see Figure 2.1) mostly had significant experience behind them, the exception being Gaye, who had only a few credits in television. This meant that they well versed to modes of low-budget film and TV production and were therefore expected to cope well with Katzman's breakneck production speed. Furthermore, Earl Barton was also an experienced jitterbug dancer (Monaghan 2008: 136) and therefore Katzman hired him to choreo- graph the dancing scenes as well as play Lisa's brother and dancing partner.

To exert full control on the production and ensure that all this talent would be integrated as well as possible with his production methods, Katzman used the same crew as in his corrupt city officials films. As mentioned already, Benjamin H. Kline took over from Henry Freulich as Katzman's main cinematographer, while the one area where the producer broke from his routine was editing. He gave the job to two

Figure 2.1 The main cast of *Rock around the Clock* consisted of actors with tenure in B film and television

Image credit: Columbia/Rex Features/Shutterstock Editorial

editors with whom he worked for the first time, Jack Ogilvie and Saul A. Goodkind. Although both had experience in B films in the previous decades, Ogilvie was also editor of Columbia's *The Eddy Duchin Story* (Sidney, 1956), a musical starring Tyrone Power as a bandleader, which proved to be the company's biggest box-office success that year. Sensing perhaps that he needed an editor with musical experience and as he had tenure in major productions, Ogilvie seemed to be a savvy choice for *RATC*.

Furthermore, the screenplay he commissioned Kent to produce was, not surprisingly, formulaic.[5] On the one hand, this allowed the screenwriters to deliver it swiftly, with reports that they 'dusted off yellowed scripts from the swing era' and presented 'the old familiar storyline [of] a music bizzer discovering a band with a "new sound." They are taken in to the "Big Time" where the act becomes an overnight sensation' (Denisoff and Romanowski 1990: 67). As noted in the Introduction, certain accounts suggested that the screenplay reworked the story of *Orchestra Wives* (Mayo, 1942), starring Glenn Miller (see Reinsch 2013: 14; Dawson 2005: 146). However, the similarities with that film are rather tenuous, with *RATC* having more in common with biopics such as *The Glenn Miller Story* and even *The Benny Goodman Story* (Davies, 1956). The latter in particular, which was released as *RATC* was being shot in January 1956, is also about a real life musician going against the grain, making music that people can dance to, appealing to young demographics, while also containing a montage sequence with trade press headlines charting the success of the musician and even a jitterbug dance scene featuring Lou Southern, one of the dancers also appearing in *RATC* (see also Chapter 4).

With the screenplay for *RATC* providing space within its narrative context for no fewer than 17 performances from the four musical attractions, it is clear that it had the potential to be produced swiftly. Citing an interview with Katzman's son Jerome, Dixon writes that the average writing period for a Katzman film script was two weeks, which was then followed by a week to 10 days for pre-production before shooting started, with that stage lasting from six days to two weeks. With the film announced on 14 November 1955 and the shooting starting on 6 January 1956 and lasting 13 days (Dawson 2005: 145), allowing for the Christmas holidays, *RATC* seems to have been a most typical Katzman production.

With the film's principal photography ending on 19 January and its theatrical release scheduled for 21 March 1956, *RATC* had approximately two months for post-production and publicity and marketing. Not surprisingly, Katzman and the Columbia distribution executives focused their energies on exploiting the title of the film, the presence of Bill Haley and His Comets and the rest of the bands that appear in it, and on highlighting rock 'n' roll as a topical, multifaceted phenomenon with literally endless angles from which it could be exploited. The film's Pressbook starts by stressing the importance of the 17 songs that appear in the film, emphasising that they were 'the nation's top rock 'n' roll tunes', but presenting them as having continuities with other well established popular music genres: 'Better 'n Boogie! Swingier 'n Swing! Jumpier 'n Jive! Bigger 'n Bob!' ('*Rock around the Clock* Pressbook' 1956: 2). 'Put it all to work', proclaims the same page as it provides exhibitors with a host of ideas for exploitation, including inviting dancing schools and ballrooms to use the music for competitive displays and offering prizes for the best local performances of the songs on radio and television (ibid.)

The Pressbook then continues with merchandise prepared specifically for the film and being available for 'theater showmen' (1956: 3). Branded hats, board games, books with the musical arrangements of the songs from the film represent typical tie-ins, while skirts for girls ('they come in junior sizes only') and T-shirts ('for the teen-age boy') represent a more concerted effort to target teenagers as the film's core demographic (ibid.). Not surprisingly, the Pressbook does not forget rock 'n' roll slang with a section on 'Slanguage' informing exhibitors that teenagers have their own language and prompting them to address their clientele in specific ways, as 'cats 'n' gators'. Suggestions to run contests through which 'a master vocabulary' can be created or the best stories in 'rock 'n' roll talk' can be told are among some of the ways that this aspect of rock 'n' roll was invited to be exploited (ibid.).

The Pressbook references the main actors Johnny Johnston and Lisa Gaye only on the last page of the publication, demonstrating further their limited value when it came to the film's publicity and exploitation. The same approach is also taken with the film's poster whereby rock 'n' roll, its stars and its key signifiers, music and dancing, take centre stage in the various designs, while the actors and the narrative are relegated to the periphery. Once again, the title of the film and Bill Haley and His Comets become the main focal point of the poster, with the latter both through the name of the band in text and a close-up of Haley's face (see the frontispiece of this book). Tag lines such as 'It's the Whole Story of Rock 'n' Roll', 'It's the Most' and 'All the Cats Are Coming to See the Screen's First Great Rock 'n' Roll Picture' accompany the various versions of the poster in a clear effort to claim authenticity for the film and connect it with the youth demographic.

Beyond this main focal point, the posters advertise the main attractions, starting with The Platters and Tony Martinez and moving to Freddie Bell and the Bellboys. Then they credit Alan Freed, before they mention the actors at the bottom of the design. All these credits are surrounded by images of musicians playing their instruments in 'action' poses and young people dancing in a jitterbug fashion. With the background of most of the designs using bright colours, especially red and yellow, everything connotes energy, excitement and exuberance, capturing fully the spirit of youthfulness and teen enthusiasm (and avoiding any connotations of rebellion and delinquency). Despite its lowly exploitation status, it is not surprising then that the film reached its core audience on its own level and, as Doherty correctly pointed out, 'to the pointed exclusion of their elders' (Doherty 1988: 74).

Conclusion

Rock around the Clock was produced and released at a point when the American film industry started to get some stability following a number of major changes that started to occur after the end of WW2.

One of these changes involved the gradual phasing out of B film production that served a very particular purpose from the beginning of the Great Depression and until the end of the 1940s and its evolution to a different type of low-budget production model that became known as exploitation film. Seeking to keep costs down by choosing subject matter that could generate free publicity, such films mined news headlines, controversial topics, fashions and fads and built stories around them. Distributors were then able to craft marketing campaigns that were cost efficient and, depending on the topic represented in the film, utilised often outlandish methods to attract the audience's attention.

Rock 'n' roll music represented the perfect subject matter for exploitation films, especially as it became connected from the start to the teen demographic that had been emerging as the most frequent cinema-going audience in 1950s America. This demographic, moreover, had become a subject of intense attention by the country's media and cultural institutions and therefore also ideal fodder for exploitation films on its own accord. By the mid-1950s, the time was right for a film that combined rock 'n' roll and youth in an explicit way, and prominent exploitation filmmaker Sam Katzman was the first one to produce such a film. Heading an established independent company with a distribution contract with Columbia allowed Katzman access to substantial resources in order to work at a great speed and to start cycles of films on particular subject matters when he thought that there was a market for them. Using a group of practitioners with huge experience in exploitation filmmaking, Katzman was able to keep a tight control of all his productions even as he was working on different subject matter film to film and cycle to cycle. His ability to secure Bill Haley and His Comets at the apex of their success for pittance and to clear the title of their most famous song for the title of the film gave Katzman a very strong foundation for what was an otherwise typical exploitation film production. By time the film was ready for release, Columbia's distribution executives had a relatively easy job to do as they used the popularity of the film's topic to attract the desired teenage audience.

However, *Rock around the Clock* was a very particular type of exploitation film that operated in a specific area of the American film industry. Rock 'n' roll and its connection to teens was also exploited by other types of companies in different ways. The next chapter will examine how *RATC* fits within the broader field of exploitation filmmaking, before Chapter 4 moves to consider how the film's narrative and style represent Katzman's particular approach to exploitation.

Notes

1 This vertical integration applied primarily to the Big Five. Columbia and Universal were only partly integrated as they did not own theatres, while United Artists was primarily a distribution company for independent producers, even though for a short period of time in the 1930s it also owned theatres (Tzioumakis 2017: 28–9).

2 Other sources bring this number much higher to 340 titles (see Staehling 1975: 222). In this book we use the number cited in the Internet Movie Database, which is 239 titles (www.imdb.com/name/nm0441947/?ref_=fn_a l_nm_1).

3 The song only spent one week in the charts at No 23.

4 In an earlier chapter in his book, Dawson states that MGM had paid $5000 for three plays of the song in *Blackboard Jungle*. A few months down the line and with the song sales in millions, it is feasible that Katzman had to pay multiple times that amount on top of the $20,000 paid to Haley and his band.

5 The script for *RATC* is credited to both Robert E. Kent and James B. Gordon. However, according to Blottner (2015: 101), Kent used often the pseudonym James B. Gordon and in some cases he credited himself as a screenwriter by using both names, perhaps to hide the fact that he was producing scripts at a breakneck speed.

3   Who's Exploiting What and How (2)

Rock around the Clock between Major Studio and Independent Film Production

This chapter continues the examination of *Rock around the Clock*'s exploitation film status by probing certain details of its production and distribution and comparing them with relevant details of the production and distribution of three other films with a similar interest: *Blackboard Jungle, Shake, Rattle and Rock!* and *Rock, Rock, Rock!*. The first represents a major Hollywood production by MGM that has not been examined through the prism of an exploitation film that tackles juvenile delinquency and targets a youth audience. Instead, *Blackboard Jungle* has been understood primarily as a social problem film, part of a film genre with a long history in Hollywood cinema, that is addressed to adults rather than teenagers.

Shake, Rattle and Rock! and *Rock, Rock, Rock!*, on the other hand, represent low-budget independent productions. The former was a film by the dominant exploitation producer-distributor of the 1950s and 1960s, American International Pictures. The latter was produced by short-lived independent production company Vanguard Productions (1956–63) and was released by the equally short-lived Distributors Corporation of America (1947–57). Made and released away from the studios these two films are of an inferior quality than both *Blackboard Jungle* and *Rock Around the Clock*. On the other hand, as we demonstrate below, their production and distribution away from the Hollywood majors provided opportunities for their makers to make some very interesting choices in terms of linking rock 'n' roll to Black music (*Shake, Rattle and Rock!*) and to present one of the first narratives revolving around the female teen experience (*Rock, Rock, Rock!*).

By comparing these four films, the chapter argues that the category of exploitation filmmaking is not a fixed or stable one and that, depending on their position in the American film industry and their access to resources, filmmakers can practise exploitation in different ways, achieving a variety of objectives. Taking a cue from Brian Taves's

DOI: 10.4324/9781315544908-4

taxonomy of the B film (Taves 1995), the chapter finishes with a similar classification of exploitation filmmaking and demonstrates the extent to which *RATC* and the other films fall under particular categories and why.

Game Changer: Slick Exploitation and *Blackboard Jungle*

Blackboard Jungle was announced as an acquisition by MGM on 13 April 1954. Written by Evan Hunter, *The Blackboard Jungle: A Novel*, as was its full title, was to be serialised by *Ladies' Home Journal* in May 1954 ('"Blackboard Jungle" …' 1954: 1), which would guarantee the novel a very strong visibility. This was because *Ladies' Home Journal* was one of the best-selling magazines in the US in 1955 with an average circulation of close to five million copies a week (Peterson 1956: 55). More importantly for MGM, the novel, which was based on the author's experience as a teacher after the end of WW2, dealt with the topic of juvenile delinquency. This was a most opportune time for a novel on that subject, not only because it was a major concern with the American public at that time. At that exact moment, on 21 April 1954, the United States Senate Subcommittee on Juvenile Delinquency started its high profile public hearings that were to last until 1956 ('1954 Senate Subcommittee …' n.d.; Gilbert 1986: 144). This meant that the novel and its potential adaptation into a major motion picture by a Hollywood studio were in prime position to *exploit* this event for publicity purposes.

At that time, MGM was managed by Dore Schary. As a liberal Democrat, Schary favoured social problem films or 'message pictures' and as a central producer for the studio he had greenlit several such films, including *Intruder in the Dust* (Brown, 1949) and *The Red Badge of Courage* (Huston, 1951) (Balio 2018: 169–70). When in the summer of 1951 he became head of MGM and at the peak of the HUAC hearings and McCarthy's power, Schary seemed to have moved away from these kinds of pictures, focusing more on the company's trademark Gene Kelly musicals and other spectacular productions. However, by the mid-1950s he had gone back to this type of films, with Balio calling this studio production trend 'message pictures redux' (187). *Bad Day at Black Rock* (Sturges), *Trial* (Robson) and *Blackboard Jungle* represent three significant such examples in 1955, all commercial successes.

It is clear then that *Blackboard Jungle* was being developed as a major studio release rather than an exploitation quickie. The film's producer, Pandro S. Berman had prior production credits in close to 100 films, including key company releases such *Ivanhoe* (Thorpe, 1952) and *The Prisoner of Zenda* (Thorpe, 1952), while other key personnel in the film included Cedric Gibbons, the legendary art director who was responsible for the production design of every major MGM film from the late 1920s to 1960. Berman had also taken time between late April and mid-June 1954 to travel to New York and do research for the film ('Pandro Berman Back' 1955: 2). Furthermore, the main parts were not cast until October and November 1954, with Dawson stating that the film started shooting in mid-November at the MGM backlot (Dawson 2005: 115). These dates confirm that the film had a substantial development period, as is usually afforded to major studio productions, which, among other things, allowed time for the production of a good script. Reinsch located the film's script with the date of 7 October 1954, which suggests that it took approximately five months to complete since the novel's acquisition in April of the same year (Reinsch 2013: 20).

On the other hand, *Blackboard Jungle* had several characteristics that bring it closer to the low-budget exploitation model of filmmaking associated with *RATC*. First and foremost, its writer-director Richard Brooks had emerged as a writer of B films at Universal in the 1940s before screenplays for well-regarded 'message pictures' such as *Brute Force* (Dassin, 1947) and *Crossfire* (Dmytryk, 1947) led to a contract as writer-director at MGM in the 1950s. At the studio, Brooks specialised in star vehicles, with the crime drama *Deadline – USA* (1952) starring Humphrey Bogart being arguably his best-known film before *Blackboard Jungle*.

He also worked with certain important members of the crew that had great experience in efficient production, especially cinematographer Russell Harlan who had made his name in B westerns before moving to major productions in the late 1940s. Significantly, Brooks and Harlan shot the film in black and white, which contributed further to its perception as a low-budget offering from a studio normally associated with Technicolor spectaculars. Similarly, editor Ferris Webster had worked primarily in MGM's B films and some undistinguished A titles, before moving to more important productions in the 1950s.

However, it was *Blackboard Jungle*'s budget and postproduction schedule that raise the most significant issues about its potential status as an exploitation film, especially as sources tend to diverge significantly in terms of how much the film cost. According to Schary, the film's budget was approximately $1,160,000 (quoted in '*Blackboard Jungle*' n.d.), which is significantly less than the $1,511,000 average for MGM films in the year prior to the film's release (Lev 2006: 14). On the other hand, Dawson cites a budget of an eye-catching $360,000

(Dawson 2005: 121) and, quoting Pandro S. Berman, outlines how *Blackboard Jungle* was conceived as a 'B movie' from the start (115). Unfortunately, Dawson does not provide sources either for the budget figure or for Berman's quote. Furthermore, given the participation of a star such as Glenn Ford and the film's six week shooting schedule (*'Blackboard Jungle'* n.d.), it is unlikely that the film would cost almost as much as a production without stars and shot over two weeks such as *RATC*. On the other hand, it is instructive that MGM refused to clear the full rights for the song 'Rock around the Clock', which would have cost $7500, opting instead to buy only synchronisation rights for three plays in the picture for the amount of $5,000 (Brooks, quoted in Doherty 1988: 204). And even though Doherty explains this 'shortsightedness' within the context of the industry's lack of readiness to 'coordinat[e] teen-oriented music and teen-targeted movies' (203), it also hardly demonstrates a company's approach to a major film production.

If these issues work to destabilise the status of *Blackboard Jungle* as a major film production, the film's change of release date from 20 May to 25 March 1955 (and later moved forward again to 19 March) provides further evidence about the extent to which it should be seen as an exploitation film. The trade press announced this change on 26 January, just a month after the end of the film's shooting ('"Anchors Aweigh" ...' 1955: 4), and confirmed that it was 'newspaper headlines and stories detailing accounts of juvenile delinquency [that had] prompted Metro to advance the release date of "The Blackboard Jungle" film dealing with this matter' ('Delinquency Theme ...' 1955: 7). Furthermore, sensing that the film may now have a solid opportunity to become a runaway success, MGM decided in mid-February to give *Blackboard Jungle* 'a special handling' ('Special Handling ...' 1955: 7). What this meant was that MGM, a studio without expertise in marketing its product to youth audiences, had understood that it was in possession of a title that could attract a significant youth demographic and therefore the company had to utilise specific marketing strategies to achieve this target.

The film's promotional texts demonstrate clearly this 'special handling'. Even a big studio, like MGM, had to look at exploitation film techniques in order to place an otherwise average-size production 'correctly' in the market, which in this case meant courting the teen audience, while ramping up the potential impact of the film to its audience more broadly. The film's trailer opens with 'Rock around the Clock' playing over a shot of Glenn Fold outside the gates of a school. As he walks towards the school the camera moves with him revealing pupils dancing and having a good time, while an enigmatic smile on his face does not make clear if he sees this as a problem or as an instance of kids blowing some steam. A few seconds later voiceover narration commences but rather than focusing on the film's star or its narrative it starts with the proclamation: 'You are now listening to "Rock around the Clock"! This is the theme music from M-G-M's sensational new picture *Blackboard Jungle*.' With MGM having no ties to Decca and therefore not benefitting financially by plugging the song, it is clear, Reinsch argues, that the decision to 'solidify' the film's link with the song (Reinsch 2013: 10) was an effort to reach the teen audience directly.

The trailer continues with more detail about the film's subject matter, making clear where it takes place, showcasing the main youth characters and highlighting the difficulty of the topic tackled. As the voiceover narration continues:

> Many people said the story could not, must not, dare not be shown; the picture has already the movie and book world gasping. *Blackboard Jungle* deals with an explosive subject, teenage terror in the schools. It is the frankest, the toughest, the most realistic film since *On the Waterfront*. It is fiction, but fiction torn from big city modern savagery. It packs a brass-knuckle punch in the startling revelation of those teenage savages who turned big city schools into a crime jungle. *Blackboard Jungle* will be the talk of this town. Don't miss it!

As this extensive narration addresses the spectator head on, the images remain firmly focused on the young cast, who overwhelm the main character (and the theatre screen) with their sheer number and through engaging in delinquent activities. It is after the end of this footage that the trailer moves to a more conventional mode that focuses on the stars and provides snippets from high impact scenes, such as fights, cars speeding and especially the attempted rape scene involving new teacher, Miss Hammond. As the trailer reaches its climax, words such as 'Shocking!' and 'Startling!' jump out of the screen, with the title of the film finally appearing imposed over a blackboard.[1] As is clear, the trailer for *Blackboard Jungle* draws directly from the exploitation film and showmanship playbook.

The same can be said for the film's poster designs, which have followed a similar approach with some looking a lot more like advertising an exploitation film than others and even at the expense of attracting teenagers in some cases. For instance, one poster centres on the attempted rape scene by including an image of Margaret Hayes screaming as a male figure covered in shadows is ready to attack her. The tagline 'The Most Startling Picture in Years!' accompanies the image, leaving little to the imagination in terms of how MGM went for the hard-selling approach (see Figure 3.1). However, the main design was a variation on a concept that highlighted most key selling points of the film: its adaptation of a best-selling novel, images of young people's delinquency, an image of Miss Hammond as 'temptation' for school pupils, and the relationship between the characters portrayed by Glenn Ford and Anne Francis with the tagline 'The Most Startling Picture of the Year' and with all this expertly placed against a bright yellow background that was not designed to be understated.[2]

Given all these exploitation strategies in the film's distribution, it is not surprising that *Blackboard Jungle* started with an exploitation-like disclaimer about its intentions to contribute to debates on the issue of teenage crime. Over the initially slow but gradually building beat of military style drums and against a black background, large white letters write:

> We, in the United States, are fortunate to have a school system that is a tribute to our communities and to our American youth. Today we are concerned with juvenile delinquency – its causes – and its effects. We are especially concerned when this delinquency boils over to our schools. The scenes and incidents depicted here are fictional. However, we believe that public awareness is a first step toward a remedy for any problem. It is in this spirit and with this faith that BLACKBOARD JUNGLE was produced.

The last beat of the drum cleverly gives way to the famous first drum beat from 'Rock around the Clock' that signals the beginning of the film's opening credits. As it is clear, and in tandem with MGM's overall marketing approach, this introduction brings the film much closer to exploitation film territory than normally assumed on account of its major studio production status. Indeed, one could argue that *Blackboard Jungle became* an exercise in exploitation filmmaking even if it may not have started as one.

Such a perspective may also complicate claims that *Blackboard Jungle*, as a major Hollywood production, conveys adult viewpoints on the teen cultures and behaviours it represents (Staehling 1975: 226; Klein 2011: 102). With young people immediately 'claiming' the film as their own on account of the disruptive power of 'Rock around the Clock' playing over the credits and the opening sequence and its

Figure 3.1 One of MGM's poster designs for *Blackboard Jungle* is a textbook
example of exploitation marketing

Image credit: MGM/Rex Features/Shutterstock Editorial

invitation to break with spectatorship decorum and start dancing (see Reinsch 2013), one can safely suggest that such adult viewpoints became secondary concerns. In this respect, we tend to agree with Leerom Medovoi's assertion that '[i]f *Blackboard's* significance had been exhausted by these "social problem" meanings, [...] it would never have become a textual prototype for the teenpic' (Medovoi 2005: 146).

Medovoi points out how the film's narrative resolution with the re-establishment of adult authority was seemingly ignored by the film's teen audiences, some of whom not only disrupted the 'social problem' message that followed the opening disclaimer by starting to dance in the aisles but also by cheering for and approving of some of the violence perpetrated by the young people on the screen (Medovoi 2005: 137–8). To this, we would like to add the film's trajectory from major studio to exploitation film production and release, which demonstrated how a film could link itself to and navigate newspaper headlines, political initiatives, cultural trends, licentious images and an emerging audience demographic under the veneer of a literary adaptation. With box-office rentals of over $5 million in the North American market alone on a budget considerably below the industry average, it is no surprise that it became the prototype for the teenpic, as Medovoi suggests. It is also no surprise that it became the prototype for exploitation tactics that would be enhanced and perfected by Katzman and other producers as the 1950s continued to unfold.

Exploiting the Exploited: *Shake, Rattle and Rock!*

Although *Rock around the Clock* was released in March 1956, the rest of the rock 'n' roll teenpics did not start to flood the screens until the end of that year. By the time it was evident that the film would be a box-office hit it was already late spring while the top rock 'n' roll stars were engaged in an intense schedule of recording and touring over the summer that made it difficult to book them for filming. While Katzman started to work on a new rock 'n' roll picture, a sort of sequel to *RATC*, again with the participation of Bill Haley and His Comets under the title *Don't Knock the Rock*, it was low-end independent company American International Pictures that was the first to jump on the rock 'n' roll teenpic bandwagon with *Shake, Rattle and Rock!*

American International Pictures was arguably the standout producer-distributor in what was becoming an exploitation film sector. It was established in 1954 under the name American Releasing Corporation by lawyer and former television producer Samuel Z. Arkoff and former theatre manager James H. Nicholson, and originally focused on 'old-style' B films. However, by 1956 it had changed its name to American International Pictures and shifted its business to serving almost exclusively the youth audience. The company also did not hide the fact that it was in the business of serving this audience by producing and releasing films that were topical and therefore highly 'exploitable', especially when it came to distribution. As Nicholson put it in an interview with the *Los Angeles Times*:

> We do our planning backwards: get what sounds like a title that will arouse interest, then a monster or gimmick; then figure what our advertising is going to consist of. Then we bring in a writer to provide a script to fit the title and concept. Now we bring in the producer – though he may have been in during the writing of the script earlier. Four of our producers are also writers and one, Corman, is also a director.
>
> (Scheuer 1958: E1)

The first pictures released under the AIP banner seemed to adhere fully to the above description, while targeting a youth audience: *Hot Rod Girl* (Martinson, 1956) and *Girls in Prison* (Cahn, 1956) were released as part of a teen-focused double bill (Betrock 1986: 24) and did spectacular business for low-end independent productions ('Low-Budget Combo ...' 1956: 11). But before these films were even released in September 1956, Nicholson had set his sight on a musical film 'aimed specifically at the teen-age and young adult group', which was announced in June of that year ('Teen-age Musical Pic' 1956: 9). With the title *Shake, Rattle and Roll* already chosen, the film would exploit Bill Haley and His Comets' song, which actually was their first chart success in the summer of 1954 (Dawson 2005: 95), before 'Rock around the Clock' got a second lease of life after its inclusion in *Blackboard Jungle* and catapulted the band into stardom. However, as Haley and his band were re-contracted by Katzman for *Don't Knock the Rock*, AIP looked at other ways through which it could exploit the highly visible song title, which had found its way in various albums, EPs and compilations as Bill Haley and His Comets' songs continued to be repackaged and recirculated in 1956.

AIP found a marketing hook in the performer who had originally recorded 'Shake, Rattle and Roll', before Bill Haley and His Comets popularised it further. That performer was 'Big Joe' Turner, who had recorded the song in February 1954, four months before Haley's version. Turner's iteration of the song had hit the No 1 spot in the R'n'B charts and had even crossed over to the *Billboard* pop charts, peaking at No 22 in April 1954 (Dawson and Propes 1992: 128, 130). Two years later, other rock 'n' roll records and acts had found bigger success and achieved greater visibility than 'Shake, Rattle and Roll'. However, the fact that Bill Haley and His Comets, who were at the peak of their popularity in the summer of 1956, had been associated with the song was sufficient for AIP to approve the title.

Turner signed with AIP to appear in the film in early August 1956 ('"Shake" Adds Musickers' 1956: 3). However, by that time the title of the film had changed to *Shake, Rattle and Rock!*, presumably because a low-end independent such as AIP was not able (or willing) to clear the rights to use the title of the song for the film's own title. But *Shake, Rattle and Rock!* was close enough, while 'Big Joe' Turner's presence in the film, no doubt, acted as a legitimating force. This was not only because of his connection with the song that was now invoked by the title but also because he was one of the main figures in the crossing over of Black rhythm 'n' blues to rock 'n' roll, as the success of his record in both R'n'B and pop charts demonstrates. And if this was not enough credibility for the film and AIP, two days prior to Turner, Nicholson had signed Antoine 'Fats' Domino, one of the most successful and influential Black solo artists in that period ('Fats Domino Signed' 1956: 8). His fee was reported as $1500 for performing three songs in the film (Gordon 1984: 30).

With the two main rock 'n' roll acts in place, the AIP production process was in full swing. A title had been chosen, rock 'n' roll music would function as a gimmick, while Domino and Turner, and the music and dancing associated with rock 'n' roll, would be the focus in the advertising campaign. Nicholson himself took on the role of the producer, which was alongside his duties as AIP chairman, and brought the screenwriter-director team of Lou Russoff and Edward L. Cahn to execute his plan. The duo had already worked together in four other AIP productions in 1956 and had internalised the company's philosophy and approach to exploitation film. The cast was a combination of stock company actors who had appeared in previous AIP productions (Touch Connors), experienced Hollywood actors who were past their peak (Sterling Holloway) and actors who had already established a presence in the emerging rock 'n' roll teenpics (Lisa Gaye). With a budget reported as an incredibly low $79,000 (Gordon, 1984: 30), *Shake, Rattle and Rock!* was ready for release just three months after its announcement in the trades (31 October), with Nicholson reportedly having hired two editors to work in shifts in order to shorten the film's post-production period as much as possible ('Two Editors' 1956: 6).

Shake, Rattle and Rock! became the first film to use the 'rock 'n' roll on trial' theme as the cornerstone of the film's narrative in an effort to exploit rock 'n' roll's alleged links to delinquency and crime but for a comedic effect. The story ridicules adult groups that are offended by rock 'n' roll and are trying to stop its organised dissemination to working-class teens by a well-meaning disc jockey, while demonstrating how the music actually helps these young people stay off the streets. The 'court' scene at the end of the film reconciles the two sides and allows the music and its young proponents to be accepted. Such a story fit well with an emerging AIP narrative formula in the 1950s that, Gary Morris argued, relied on portraying 'teenagers and other socially unempowered groups and their inability to assimilate into a society whose conventions (conformity, ambition) they ridiculed and rejected' (Morris 1993: 4). Such a formula had the advantage of placing teenagers consciously at the forefront of the narrative, with their way of life, style and problems also brought centre stage.

In true exploitation manner, this story was interspersed with performances by the two main attractions of classic songs such as 'Ain't that a Shame' by Fats Domino and 'Feelin' Happy' by Joe Turner, while several scenes with dancing teens accompanied some of these performances. And even though neither Domino nor Turner (who appeared under their real names) were integrated in the narrative in the way Bill Haley and His Comets were in *RATC*, they both had some interaction with the fictional characters, with Domino in particular acknowledging his diegetic teen fans before rehearsing a song in front of them. Finally, as perhaps the strongest evidence of the ways in which AIP exploited the already exploited, the film finishes with the phrase 'The Most ... to Say the Least ...' as a response to *RATC*'s end phrase 'The Living End'.

Taking another chapter from the *Rock around the Clock* exploitation playbook, while also nodding to *Blackboard Jungle*, AIP's marketing approach emphasised the youthful energy associated with (the gimmick of) rock 'n' roll, with images of couples dancing in acrobatic style dominating the imagery of the poster.[3] Set against a bright yellow background, the images strongly anchor the film's title. The names of the music acts are also mentioned, alongside the titles of some of the songs performed in the film. Again, like *RATC*, the names of the actors are pushed to the background, demonstrating who the real stars of *Shake, Rattle and Rock!* were. Finally, the poster employed two taglines, one providing a hook for the film's narrative ('rock 'n' roll vs the "squares"') and the other promising a spectacle of music and dancing ('the rockin', rollin', boppingest jam session you've ever seen!').

If this was not enough to entice teenage audiences, AIP paired *Shake, Rattle and Rock!* with another teen-targeting film, *Runaway*

Daughters (Cahn, 1956) (Betrock 1986: 24) and released them as a double bill. Written and directed by the same duo responsible for *Shake, Rattle and Rock!*, *Runaway Daughters* was a conventional juvenile delinquency teenpic, the marketing for which tried to evoke the licentious and the depraved, with the tagline 'They called her "Jailbait"' accompanying the image of three young girls silhouetted on a pitch black background and running away from a dead body. Such a release strategy seems to have been effective. Speaking specifically about *Shake, Rattle and Rock!*, Nicholson claimed that the rock 'n' roll teenpic played in over 3000 theatres in the two month period following its release and the expectation was that it would reach 10,000 playdates and become the most widely released film in AIP's history ('"Shake, Rattle ..." 1956: 2).

AIP's no-frills approach to filmmaking, its working with very low budgets and its commitment to the rules of exploitation filmmaking often allowed it to make films that provided a platform for the voices of underrepresented groups to be heard. In the case of *Shake, Rattle and Rock!* this was literally through the appearance of Turner and Domino, whose strong presence and repeated performances go a long way to highlight rock 'n' roll's roots in Black rhythm and blues as opposed to *Rock around the Clock* that all but erases this heritage. The above-mentioned scene of Domino rehearsing a song in front of a White teen audience creates huge

Figure 3.2 Fats Domino interacts with White teen fans in *Shake, Rattle and Rock!*

excitement in them, while Domino addresses the group face to face before his rehearsal in ways that also go a long way to 'normalise' race relations in mid-1950s America (see Figure 3.2).

If in the previous decades some B films had taken the option to target under-represented and under-served audiences in terms of class, ethnicity and race (Tzioumakis 2017: 70), the exploitation independents of the 1950s continued to function in a similar way. However, they also shifted the medium's attention to yet another previously ignored demographic, the youth audience, helping American cinema to be even more inclusive in terms of the clientele it catered for. Indeed, the lower one goes in terms of budget and production values and the further away from the studios in terms of approach to filmmaking, the more opportunities one can find both for creative exploitation and, arguably, transgressive potential as the last case study of this chapter demonstrates.

Bargain-Basement Exploitation: *Rock, Rock, Rock!*

The third film to jump on the rock 'n' roll bandwagon was big studio production *The Girl Can't Help It* (Tashlin), which was released on 1 December 1956. Also utilising the visibility and success of a well-known song for its title, Little Richard's 'The Girl Can't Help It', the film stands as a strange example of a picture that did not attempt to directly exploit rock 'n' roll. Instead, its narrative is built on a variation of the old-fashioned story of a rich man who wants to launch the career of his young but untalented girlfriend, before becoming clear that the priorities of both characters lie elsewhere. The efforts to turn the young woman into a professional singer provide many opportunities for musical performances by some of the best-known rock 'n' roll acts of the time (Gene Vincent, Eddie Cochran, Little Richard, Fats Domino, The Platters, among others). This is a surprising choice given that both the style of music that the young woman is promoted for (light pop, including a parody of 'Rock around the Clock' under the title 'Rock around the Rock Pile') and the overall aesthetic of the film (shot in Technicolor and CinemaScope) suggest that the film has more in common with classic musicals rather than jukebox musicals/rock 'n' roll teenpics. An awkward mix of exploitation and old-style Hollywood, *The Girl Can't Help It* received mixed reviews, while its commercial success was modest, with Aubrey Solomon reporting that it returned domestic rentals of $2.8 million on a budget of $1.3 million (Solomon 1988: 251, 227).

It is the film that was released a week later, on 8 December 1956, however, that is the focus of this section. Unlike all the other films mentioned above, *Rock, Rock, Rock!* was the only one to not use the title of a pre-existing song as its title.[4] It was also a film that was not made by a seasoned exploitation film producer, such as Sam Katzman, or a new company with an identity in the exploitation marketplace, such as AIP. Instead *Rock, Rock, Rock!* was made by a new company, Vanguard Productions, that had not produced any pictures prior to that time (and that would prove to be a short-lived outfit that folded in 1963). The film's two producers, Max Rosenberg and Milton Subotsky, had only one prior credit each, both on the same television show, *Junior Science* (1954), while one of them, Subotsky, doubled in the film as a screenwriter having only a handful of writing credits in television. The director, Will Price, had directed only two feature films prior to *Rock, Rock, Rock!*, with the most recent one released several years earlier, in 1950. Finally, the film's protagonists were 13-year-old Tuesday Weld, in the first role of her career, and Teddy Randazzo, a member of vocal harmony group The Three Chuckles, which had only minor hits in the charts.

The above details suggest that *Rock, Rock, Rock!* was a rather opportunistic project that was put together by people with little experience in filmmaking. However, reading correctly the trends in American popular culture, they had understood that there was enough space in the marketplace for yet another rock 'n' roll-themed film that could prove successful with teen audiences. Announcing the production in August 1956, the trade press reported that the film would be shot in a small studio in Bronx, NY, with a budget of approximately $80,000 and a two-week shooting schedule. Its distribution would be handled by another new company, Distributors Corporation of America, which was established in 1954 with a view to releasing foreign film imports and low-budget US independent productions ('Self Help' 1954: 5).

However, further reports in the trade press of the time suggest that the film was a vehicle for a complex and highly lucrative business deal involving Alan Freed. Not only did the prominent disc jockey participate in the film as a master of ceremonies introducing musical performances (his name appears first in the opening credits), he was also an investor in the production with a 10% participation (Bundy 1956: 16). Furthermore, his music publishing company Snapper Music controlled the publishing rights of 15 of the 21 songs in the film's score, while he also stood to collect 'BMI performance credits, via a unique deejay promotion of the picture' (ibid.).[5] Finally, his agreement also included live appearances in the New York theatres playing the film (30).

On 24 November 1956, two weeks before the film's release, Freed sold Snapper Music to the publishing company Kahl & Levy. The latter already controlled the rights to the rest of the songs that were heard in the film and was now empowered to make a number of deals, such as authorising pop covers of certain rock 'n' roll songs that appear in the film and making a deal with major label Chess Records for a compilation album under the title *Rock, Rock, Rock!*, which would feature songs of the three best known artists appearing in the film (Chuck Berry, The Moonglows and The Flamingos), but not necessarily with just the songs that are heard in the film ('Kahl & Levy' 1956: 15). In doing this, *Rock, Rock, Rock!* has been credited as the first compilation album tied in to a film (Dellar 2019: 126).

With all those deals taking place behind the scenes it is not surprising that the film itself is firmly a secondary concern. Reviewed by *Billboard* critics, *Rock, Rock, Rock!* was perceived as nothing more than a 'successful translation of the rock and roll revues Freed [had] been producing in the [previous] few years into the cinema idiom' (Kramer 1956: 22). The reviewer continues by calling the story a 'frail framework which is all but lost in the parade of acts' and admitting that 'it's hard for [its] teenage actors [...] to vie for attention in competition with a fire-ball like young Frankie Lymon or master showman Chuck Berry' (ibid.). The reviewer is right. Unlike in other rock 'n' roll films where performances are interspersed throughout the narrative, in *Rock, Rock, Rock!* they tend to be clustered in long sequences (with two 17-minute sequences at the beginning and the end of the film containing six and seven performances, respectively). For this reason, by the time the film returns to the narrative, audiences need time to remember what was happening prior to this outburst of rock 'n' roll music.

The film trade press, on the other hand, was much more direct and harsher in its views about the film. The *Variety* reviewer labelled the film as being 'of lesser quality' compared to other pictures addressed to teens, called the musical acts that appear in it 'unimpressive' (with the exception of LaVern Baker and Chuck Berry) and the film's plot 'mediocre'. However, it is the production aspects of the film that attracted the reviewer's more acerbic comments: 'sound recording is unusually bad', Alan Freed's band 'can't even play good r'n'r. Some of the turns are so incredibly bad', 'lensing, editing and other technical credits are below grade' (Brog 1956: 6).

And yet *Rock, Rock, Rock!* also proved a commercial success, especially given its shoestring budget. A July 1957 *Variety* article reported that the film was expected to reach 10,000 playdates (just like *Shake, Rattle and Rock!*), while Distributors Corporation of America projected that the film would record a box-office gross of $800,000 in the North American market alone ('It Was a Bumpy ...' 1957: 24). And this would be on top of other significant profits for the film's various investors from the exploitation of its music in the ancillary markets.

However, where this bargain-basement exploitation film may have been able to transcend its limitations and claim an important position in the rock 'n' roll film cycle and the teenpic more broadly is both on account of the breadth of Black talent it showcases and the fact that its otherwise 'frail' story squarely focuses on the everyday problems and issues of 1950s teens, in particular teen girls. In terms of the former, and despite being labelled 'unimpressive', *Rock, Rock, Rock!* boasts the presence of five Black acts performing seven songs in their entirety, ranging from doo wop to classic R'n'B and Chuck Berry's trademark rock 'n' roll guitar sound. This is arguably the most extensive presence of Black musicians in a teenpic in the 1950s and once again evidence about the range of opportunities that exist in the low-end independent sector away from the Hollywood studios.

In terms of the latter, the condensed narrative focuses on high school girl Dori (Tuesday Weld) and her efforts to find the money she needs to buy a beautiful gown to go to the prom with popular high school boy singer Tommy (Teddy Randazzo). This narrative is played out in scenes where Dori tries to convince her father to give her the money, where she tries to make the money through an elaborate borrowing and lending money scheme at high school, through fights she has with other fellow pupils and, indeed, through 'integrated' singing numbers (where Weld is dubbed by Connie Francis) that give the audience access to her thoughts and feelings through the form of the ballad. With all the other rock 'n' roll films taking drastically different and often fantastic narrative lines (such as the rock 'n' roll trials of *Don't Knock the Rock* and *Shake, Rattle and Rock!*), one could argue that *Rock, Rock, Rock!* is more grounded to the teen experience than the other films of that particular cycle. Its high school setting, the female protagonist's narrative goal, her relationship with other pupils, friends and her parents, her leisure time that is spent on watching rock 'n' roll on television and calling her friends, her pocket money spending habits (which motivate part of the narrative) and many other elements are part of an iconography that would characterise what would become the teen film in later decades (see Figure 3.3).

Equally importantly, the main part is played by a 13-year-old actress, a rare representation of an actual teenager portraying a teenager, while the film's narrative emphasis on a teenage girl (rather than a boy) in a film selling rock 'n' roll represents another potentially transgressive element, given rock 'n' roll's association with masculinity and boys' cultures. In other words, *Rock, Rock, Rock!*'s bargain-basement exploitation filmmaking, by

Figure 3.3 13-year-old Tuesday Weld represents a rare example of an actual teen girl in *Rock, Rock, Rock!*

accident or by design, has been able to use its limitations to highlight even more strongly than other rock 'n' roll teenpics the Black roots of the music while at the same time come up with a story that introduces a number of elements that will become staples of a genre.

Conclusion: The Four Faces of Exploitation

In his influential account of the B film in the studio era, Brian Taves presented a taxonomy of B films based on the companies that produced and released them, and their function in US film exhibition:

a   major-studio 'programmers'
b   major-studio B's
c   smaller-company B's
d   the quickies of the Poverty Row (Taves 1995: 317).

He labels major-studio 'programmers' films that were either A or B and which often could take either place in the double bill, depending on the exhibition arrangement (ibid.). While the budgets of these films could often be quite high, 'they never attain[ed] the aura of prestige associated with the high gloss of the A movie' (ibid.). Studio B's, on the other hand, were films produced to meet exhibition needs of the studios' theatres and, arguably more importantly, to '[keep] facilities and contract talent constantly busy' (318). Such films often had a 'house style' depending on the studio (ibid.) and their budgets tended to be both low and stable, which enabled the organisation to practise efficient production. Smaller-company B's were made by low-end independents that 'commanded respect within the industry' (321). The quality of such productions tended to be inferior to the major-studio B's (ibid.) but superior to the final category, which included films made by companies of a 'transitory nature' that 'lack[ed] finance' and had 'limited access to necessary facilities and equipment' (323). Such films, Taves asserts, 'usually received one or two reviews at most in the trades, and often none at all' (ibid.).

We conclude this chapter by adopting and adapting this taxonomy for the purposes of understanding the gradation of exploitation filmmaking in 1950s America, and propose that *Blackboard Jungle*, *Rock around the Clock*, *Shake, Rattle and Rock!* and *Rock, Rock, Rock!* represent four distinct categories of exploitation cinema. These categories could be labelled as:

a   major-studio (often latent) exploitation films
b   major-studio/low-end independent exploitation films
c   low-end independent exploitation films
d   bargain-basement exploitation films.

Blackboard Jungle and *The Girl Can't Help It* represent examples of the first category. Neither film had a major Hollywood star (with Glenn Ford and Tom Ewell being respectable and reliable performers rather than film anchoring stars) and their budgets were below the industry average. In both cases the narrative represents an old-fashioned story (a teacher tries to succeed in a tough school while keeping his marriage going; a gangster hires an impresario to help him launch the singing career of his young girlfriend). However, the films' production in the mid-1950s put them into contact with the emerging rock 'n' roll music and culture, which found their way through the choice of music and the focus on juvenile delinquency in the classroom in the former and the (unintegrated) musical performances in the latter. Both films were still perceived as Hollywood studio productions that were not necessarily made with a youth audience in mind, despite the fact that *Blackboard Jungle*'s publicity in particular ensured that it targets that audience directly. However, they were both 'hijacked' by young people who chose to ignore the films' messages or their key themes, opting instead to concentrate on the rock 'n' roll music that is heard/performed in them.

Rock around the Clock represents a clear example of an exploitation film made as part of a studio collaboration with a low-end independent. Finding its stride as a major studio after WW2, Columbia

Pictures continued its low-budget production through in-house and independent producers who were working at a breakneck speed to produce films on topical and often sensational matters. Sam Katzman was arguably the most experienced of such producers and his instincts turned him to rock 'n' roll as a topical cultural trend that could be exploited. Having had success with films dramatising other topical issues, he produced *RATC* in a matter of weeks for approximately $300,000. The film exploited specifically the success of the song 'Rock around the Clock', which had been *Blackboard Jungle*'s main attraction for young people, and paved the way for a cycle of rock 'n' roll related films made both by his company for Columbia and other outfits with no corporate links to the studios.

One such outfit was American International Pictures, producer and distributor of *Shake, Rattle and Rock!*, a low-end independent exploitation film. With budgets in the $100,000 mark and no major studio to release its films, AIP specialised in mining topical subjects for its films which would help the company's well-oiled marketing machine sell them to the youth demographic. *Shake, Rattle and Rock!* took a number of elements from Katzman's approach to exploitation filmmaking. However, AIP also developed its own strategies, including the teenpic double bill, which enabled it to assert its place in that particular marketplace and earn the respect of the industry. The company's approach to targeting teens also often enabled it to produce and release films that were relevant to that group and provided attractions that may not be able to be found in the studios' films.

Finally, *Rock, Rock, Rock!* represents an example of the bargain-basement exploitation film, a quickie made to cash in on a fad or other topical subject by parties that moved opportunistically and with little concern about the quality of the final product. Indeed, in this particular case the final product was of a decidedly low technical quality. However, as our analysis demonstrated, the film was not the main business focus of the deal that created it and was rather a promotion vehicle for rock 'n' roll DJ Alan Freed and the bands represented by his publishing company. But even in this turf, far away from the filmmaking practices of the major studios, a film such as *Rock, Rock, Rock!* had legitimating features that enabled it to transcend its otherwise bargain-basement exploitation film status. These features included both the breadth of the Black performers who appeared in it and its foundational contribution to the teen film genre more broadly.

Chapter 4 turns its attention to stylistic and narrative elements in *Rock around the Clock* with a view to determining how exploitation filmmaking may operate on an aesthetic level. As our analysis will show, *Rock around the Clock* is a complex film aesthetically, while also characterised by unusual levels of self-reflexivity that, among other things, help viewers understand the ways in which exploitation works.

Notes

1 The trailer is available at www.youtube.com/watch?v=xnK_G2IboSY.
2 The poster is available at https://movieposters.ha.com/itm/movie-posters/drama/blackboard-jungle-mgm-1955-half-sheet-22-x-28-style-a-drama/a/161741-52028.s.
3 The poster can be found at https://m.imdb.com/title/tt0049749/mediaviewer/rm1093696768.
4 The song 'Rock, Rock, Rock!' heard in the film was written specifically for it.
5 BMI (short for Broadcast Music, Inc.) is a performance rights management organisation that collects royalties for its members. In the 1950s it tended to represent the majority of rock 'n' roll artists (especially Black ones) as opposed to ASCAP (short for American Society of Composers, Authors and Publishers), which represented the major labels and established musicians. See also Introduction.

4 Who's Exploiting What and How (3)

Film Adaptation and the Boundaries of Exploitation in *Rock around the Clock*

In an article that examines the relationship between film adaptation and exploitation, I.Q. Hunter makes a convincing argument that sees the latter as 'a mode' of the former (Hunter 2009: 8), labelling exploitation 'a minor, left-handed form of adaptation' and, provocatively, calling it 'adaptation's shadowy Other' (10). Hunter bases his argument on recent work on film adaptation that also considers films derived from 'non-literary sources', such as theme park rides, trade cards and comics. Such work tends to emphasise questions of 'intertextuality over fidelity' and perceives adaptation as part of long-established film industry practices that 'spin out and recycle narratives', disseminating them across various media, especially in today's highly converged media environment (8). In this line of thought, adaptation can be likened to other industry practices and methods of production, such as genre and stardom, which[enable film producers to 'standardiz[e] production and repackage the familiar within an economy of sameness and difference' (9). Looking at adaptation in this way, 'as a rational commercial strategy for commodifying textual material', Hunter argues, makes it very difficult to find any film that 'is not involved in a relation of adaptation' (8). It is also very difficult to find a film that is '*only* an adaptation' (9, emphasis in the original) and not participate in other networks of relations with other films and other media.

From this foundation, Hunter moves to approach exploitation as a similar method of standardising production. Starting from Doherty's account of 'classical exploitation' of the period from 1920 to the 1950s, and its evolution into the 1950s teenpics, Hunter shifts the emphasis somewhat to how such films often 'explicitly imitate other movies, cannibalizing their titles, concepts and publicity gimmicks' (Hunter 2009: 9). This enables sometimes the emergence of a tightly defined cycle of films but also of films that tend to borrow 'the most exploitable elements of a specific high profile movie' (ibid.). Indeed, Hunter

DOI: 10.4324/9781315544908-5

continues, exploitation films 'may borrow little more than a title, concept and poster design' but 'that is more than enough to secure a
potentially lucrative association with the original' (ibid.). Seen from
this perspective, exploitation is a form of imitation, which is a standard
practice in film and other media. This, of course, includes the Hollywood film industry which was built on production practices that utilised genre and stardom, both involved in what Hunter calls 'the
economical reuse of preexisting narrative resources' (10). Where
exploitation seems to differ is in the subject matter of such films, the
low budgets afforded to them and the fact that it has been practised
primarily (though not exclusively) by independent producers and distributors (ibid.).

As the next section will demonstrate, quite a few aspects of Hunter's
work can be productively utilised to understand *Rock around the
Clock*, not only as an exploitation film but also as an adaptation (of a
song, of the story of a band's road to success, of the story of how rock
'n' roll emerged as a major new sound, among others). However, before
embarking on this analysis, it is important to understand how adaptation of non-literary sources operates and how it can be approached.
Thomas Leitch's work on 'postliterary adaptation' (Leitch 2009) is
particularly helpful to understand both these aspects, while Ian Inglis's
focus on how songs are used in films (Inglis 2012) raises important
questions about the extent to which they can be adapted. Furthermore,
Inglis's earlier work on the rock biopic (Inglis 2007) provides an interesting context through which to link adaptation to issues relating to
exploitation. Together, these sources provide a strong framework
through which one can understand *Rock around the Clock* as, what we
call, 'exploitative adaptation'.

Leitch starts from the idea that there has been a literary and narrative bias in adaptation studies at the expense of non-literary sources
and asserts that postliterary adaptation renders the issue of fidelity as
irrelevant, allowing scholars to see the phenomenon of adaptation in
new light. One particularly important, for the purposes of this book,
issue he identifies is the extent to which a cinematic adaptation of a
non-literary text trades in 'the marketing aura of the original' (Leitch
2009: 260). In other words, the adaptation does not necessarily occupy
itself with the textual elements of a prior text but with the marketing
possibilities that the prior text generates, which serve different purposes
and reach audiences in the new medium in different ways. Leitch is
also quick to highlight that such adaptations can only borrow a 'ske-
letal outline' from the earlier text, with the rest of the narrative developed in a number of ways. For instance, it can be filled through the

'playful use of familiar elements from the original source whose recognition in a new context will evoke pleasure;' through 'the activation of narrative potentialities already implicit in the source text;' through utilising 'circumstantial detail by evoking resonant historical settings;' through drawing on earlier narrative texts and utilising genre conventions; and, importantly, through a 'generally and often incongruously lightsome tone suggesting that this sort of adaptation is fundamentally more whimsical than the serious adaptation of novels or plays or stories' (262).

Although Leitch did not make any references to adaptations of songs, Inglis concentrates exclusively on music and songs as source material for films. He starts by acknowledging how different such a form of adaptation is from the 'standard' understanding of adaptation from a literary source, pointing out that in the latter case, the contents of the source 'are invariably reduced in size to satisfy the demands of the screenplay', whereas in the former they 'are invariably expanded' (Inglis 2012: 312). He places this type of adaptation within a long history of a relationship between music and film that is characterised by both aesthetic and commercial links and identifies several practices through which such links have materialised (313). The first involves a variety of forms through which pop stars and/or their music is the main subject of the films. This includes the recasting of pop stars as movie stars in musicals or films with a strong music focus; narrative films in which popular music provides the main context; biopics of pop stars; and even films where the score is driven by pre-existing tracks (ibid.). As we will see in the next section, *RATC* draws on a number of such practices generously.

The second main practice involves 'the adaptation of music itself into movies' (Inglis 2012: 313–4). In the first instance, this related to the routine use of a song title as a film title, with 'often little acknowledgement of the song's presence other than use as incidental background music and/or its reprise over the end credits' (314). Inglis notes that such a practice emerged mostly in the 1980s and 1990s with films using older 'classic' songs in an effort to mobilise feelings of nostalgia and appeal to the baby boom audience (ibid.). More recently, however, films like *Mamma Mia!* (Lloyd, 2008) have taken this practice to a different direction by using the songs of one band or performer in a fictional narrative and in relation to character motivation or psychology (ibid.). Again, *Rock around the Clock* utilises this practice in interesting ways, being the first film to *adapt* 'rock 'n' roll music into film, to 'turn a song into a film', as James (2016: 33) put it, and, indeed, to use eight other performances of songs by the same band in the film.

The third practice involves the adaptation of pre-existing albums into films, with concept albums by The Beatles, The Who, David Bowie and Pink Floyd being prominent examples of this trend (Inglis 2012: 315–6). Finally, Inglis identifies the adaptation of a song's lyrics into a film, a practice that demonstrates a number of complexities and has an interesting history. Inglis cites examples that include 'The Yellow Submarine', 'Alice's Restaurant' and 'Ode to Billy Joe', stating that these songs give the films that were based on them 'the themes introduced in the original song' (317). However, he is also quick to add that such a practice has a very distinctive past in Hollywood cinema, with songs that appeared in particular films acting as sources for new films (for instance, 'Singin' in the Rain' in *The Hollywood Revue of 1929* [Reisner] became the basis for *Singin' in the Rain* [Donen and Kelly, 1952]). In such cases, Inglis argues, the songs contributed little to the narrative, apart from the provision of an indicative setting but, at the same time, the broadly romantic sentiments embodied in the lyrics (and titles) worked to introduce audiences to the films' overarching themes.

As we see in the next section, *RATC* draws from both the adaptation of music and songs by Bill Haley and His Comets and the pre-existing song 'Rock around the Clock' (Inglis's categories two and four), while also employing a number of tropes that fall under his first category. Not surprisingly, this multiple practice adaptation project makes for a complex new text that stands as a fascinating example of the productive ways in which exploitation intersects with adaptation. Before the ensuing analysis shows how exactly all these elements combine in *RATC*, we need one more building block that is necessary for understanding the film as an adaptation: adaptation's relationship to the biopic, especially its subcategory of the pop/rock biopic, also examined by Inglis (2007).

Inglis uses the opening pages of that work to explain why pop/rock biopics tend to be ignored by academic criticism. He cites a number of issues, including their participation in other genres too (which makes their precise categorisation difficult), the tendency to present predictable, sanitized and hagiographic accounts of the lives of pop stars mostly within low-budget films that rarely try to make an artistic statement and an inherent elitism in academia which often privileges other types of music biopics (classical musicians) and affords them more respect than pop music (Inglis 2007: 79–82). This leads him to question what pop/rock music biopics 'seek to do', and he provides three possible answers, all of which can be seen as important for a film like *Rock around the Clock*:

a present an accurate picture of reality, a more or less plausible account of historical events.

b fabricate a version of history that may be subjective, idiosyncratic, prejudiced.

c fashion a commercially attractive product in which questions of accuracy and evidence are actually seen as irrelevant.

(Inglis 2007: 83)

Inglis then provides examples of biopics that have invented situations, displaced or elided important characters and provided interpretation of events that go against musicians' memoirs or biographical accounts. On the other hand, he acknowledges that quite often these films tend to be a primary source for understanding the life and work of particular musicians, especially for people who do not have a strong attachment to their music (Inglis 2007: 85–6). In the end, he argues, the key issue is that such texts are *not* made for 'historical accuracy and literal truth' but for entertainment and commercial success and their point of view is always filtered by factors such as studio style, stardom, genre conventions, etc. (88). Inglis then provides an interesting filter through which biopics can be approached, depending on who performs the songs in the film (ranging from the artists themselves to actors miming to original recordings, to actors re-recording and singing original songs to actors miming someone else's re-recordings of original songs – with each one being further removed from the original) (88–9), which raises a number of interesting questions about truth and fiction.

Unlike in his work on the adaptation of popular songs, Inglis is not interested here in questions of adaptation and how they may relate to the biopic. He does, however, admit that biopics often 'adapt and amend' fragments from original sources in an effort to make them fit together in a two-hour treatment that needs to be linear in terms of time and present 'a plausible sequence of events within an attractive and accessible framework' (Inglis 2007: 85). Approaching them in this manner, biopics certainly represent yet another category of adaptation and, not surprisingly, provide another frame to understand *RATC*.

Indeed, besides (arguably) adapting 'Rock around the Clock' and the music of Bill Haley and His Comets, the film may also present (a version of) the history of the band and its meteoric rise to success. Such a version may represent a 'plausible account of historical events' (further legitimated by the presence in the film of Bill Haley and His Comets as well as real-life DJ and rock 'n' roll advocate Alan Freed), especially for audiences not following the music scene, but also one that is 'fabricated' and 'prejudiced' (especially on account of eliding rock 'n' roll's relationship with rhythm and blues and Black performers). At the same time, it also presents such an account as part of a 'commercially attractive product in which questions of accuracy and evidence are [...] irrelevant', especially as the target audience for the film was teenagers and not music connoisseurs. It is clear then that *Rock around the Clock* can also be considered a biopic, next to an adaptation of a song while also being an example of exploitation film that is about the art (and the business of) exploitation. It is the last aspect that the next section will focus on before delving on questions about adaptation.

The Art of Exploitation

The film's narrative starts with Steve Hollis (Johnny Johnston), a big band manager, realising that the time of swing, as a popular music to dance to, is over. Standing in front of an almost empty dance hall (see Figure 4.1) and seeing the band that he manages playing an orchestral version of 'Let's Fall in Love' without energy or spirit, and the band leader angry about the situation,[1] Steve delivers the news that the band has been cancelled out in this town. George Hiller, the band leader, immediately protests the news, which motivates an exchange between the two men about the state of big band music. George believes that the cancellation is the manager's fault as he booked the band in a town (without naming it) where this kind of music is not drawing crowds. Steve, on the other hand, thinks that the cancellation is the result of a clear trend that had been established for some time and about which he

Figure 4.1 Big band music is dead and Steve Hollis knows it

had warned the band leader 'a long time ago:' big bands are breaking up; people are not dancing any more but instead prefer to listen to records; or, if they go out, they opt to see and listen to 'small groups, vocalists, novelty combos'. George disagrees and once again blames Steve for doing a bad job as a manager. But the latter continues to counter the band leader with the authority of someone who has studied the music market and understands how it is shifting. He makes references to record sales (without being more specific) and asserts that the band leader should move with the times, which prompts George to fire his manager.

Although Steve is not providing any details or examples to back up his views, a quick look at the trade press of the time can be very revealing as to whether he is correct or not. In a survey of 'show biz' in 1953, *Variety* highlighted how the public has become increasingly 'sound conscious', while 'high fidelity' has emerged as a very important aspect in the music industry, both in terms of record production and in terms of hi-fi equipment which are now mass marketed (Green 1954: 59). Later in 1954, *Billboard* reported on how 'Hot lick crews [have been] muscling out big bands in many territorial spots', stating how 'the money which was once spent on large dance bands is now paying for jazz groups and showmanship musicians' (Schickel 1954: 20). Finally, on 15 October 1955, a month before the announcement of *Rock around the Clock* in the trade press, *Billboard* ran an editorial under the title: 'Tin Pan Alley Fade on Pop Music Broader Horizons'. Taking as its starting point the continuing impact of rhythm and blues on mainstream pop music and acknowledging that this is a pattern that has been 'coming into focus for some years', the article suggests that pop music has been 'broadening', with novelty acts, country and western music and rhythm and blues all threatening Tin Pan Alley's role as 'song purveyor to the nation' (Ackerman 1955: 1, 16).

One can almost visualise Sam Katzman reading the trades and making notes of such articles to stay ahead of the curve and continue to get ideas for his films. Whether this narrative frame was devised by Katzman or the screenwriters, it is clear that it represents topical subject matter that will motivate the appearance of rock 'n' roll, another topical subject matter that will be the focus of the film's exploitation. Indeed, in framing the narrative in this way, *Rock around the Clock* opens up two key questions: (a) whether Steve is correct, in which case the audience expects to see him involved with and representing the 'right' kind of talent; and (b) whether he has been managing George Hiller (whose name and whose band's trademark are very similar to those of Glenn Miller) and his band badly, and therefore he needs to change his approach to management. As the narrative moves to the next scene, it appears that Steve may be a bad manager and incorrect in his understanding of the music business. Arriving at the fictional small town of Strawberry Springs, he is confronted with the picture of hordes of young people going to a dance at the town hall on Saturday night. Worse, the motel owner in which Steve and sidekick (former George Hiller band cellist) Corny LaSalle are staying for the night, confirms that the Saturday dance is a staple in the town's night life, which goes completely against Steve's understanding of the market.

However, Steve is not quick to admit that he is wrong. If anything, he thinks the whole town (just like George) is not up to date with trends in the rest of the country, especially as it seems to be in the middle of nowhere. Strawberry Springs is a fictional town and the narrative is at pains not to make any concrete references that would locate the place in which Steve would soon 'discover' rock 'n' roll. Despite his strong convictions, Steve decides to check out the dance in order to find out what motivated young people to take part in it. This brings him into his first contact with rock 'n' roll in the shape of 'See You Later, Alligator', which is being performed by Bill Haley and His Comets as Steve and Corny arrive at the town hall. Although the film opened with 'Rock around the Clock' playing over the credits, the makers of the film chose to introduce the band visually with a brand-new single that had been launched in January 1956 and was still going strong in the charts by the end of March when the film was released. The song can be heard before Steve and Corny enter the town hall, with Corny describing it as 'slaughtering cattle' after assuming that the music would be played by the 'Joe Grabneck and His Makes You Wanna Sit This One Out Orchestra'. Steve, however, remains curious and the two men enter the town hall.

At this point, the camera leaves Steve's perspective and adopts a more 'objective' point of view by looking at the stage and dance floor through a high angle shot revealing a dozen couples doing the jitterbug with the band barely seen at the background of the frame (see Figure 4.2). By doing this, the makers of the film distance the introduction of rock 'n' roll from Steve's adult perspective that had been the viewers' guide to the narrative, ensuring that the targeted teen demographic gets to listen to the music and experience the dancing without being attached to any adult gaze, while at the same time providing a spectacular – for the size of the production – first image of rock 'n' roll. It takes another four shots for Steve and Corny to literally walk on to the frame from behind the camera and see with their own eyes what viewers had already been experiencing. As they stand in front of the dancing crowd with their backs at the

Figure 4.2 An 'objective', adult-perspective-free introduction of rock 'n' roll for the film's target demographic

camera, they start discussing what they see and try to get answers from a euphoric female dancer who lets them into the secret that all young viewers are already aware of: 'it's rock 'n' roll, brother, and we are rockin' tonight'.

This is by far the longest shot for the duration of the song (approximately 35 seconds out of 3 minutes) and its function is to demonstrate how cut off from youth cultures adults are or, conversely, how little teenagers have in common with adult cultures. With Steve and Corny trying to figure out how it is related to established genres of popular music such as boogie, swing and jive and professing that it is an amalgam of these, one can imagine how the young audience of the film would find this conversation comedic. Taking this shot away, the rest of the song consists of 32 shots over two minutes and 25 seconds for a 4.5 second average shot length, which suggests a fast edited scene that strongly befits the tempo of the music. Furthermore, the editing uses a variety of shots, high angle (capturing the action), floor level (focusing on the dancers' steps), shots of Haley and the band (capturing the rock 'n' roll stars and their performance as they play their instruments and sing) and eye level shots of the dancefloor (focusing on the dancing and the energy and spirit of the young people as well as Steve and Corny's efforts to find out more about the music). The combination of all these camera levels, angles and distances creates an arresting scene that provides an introduction proper to rock 'n' roll in the way that satisfies the young audiences (see Figures 4.3–4.6).

Figure 4.3 An introduction proper to rock 'n' roll from a variety of angles and perspectives

Figure 4.4 An introduction proper to rock 'n' roll from a variety of angles and perspectives

Following the end of the song, Steve meets Bill Haley and finds out the name of the band, before the second rock 'n' roll performance of the film takes place. Only 30 seconds after the end of 'Alligator', 'Rock-A-Beatin' Boogie' represents a different kind of spectacle as it introduces Lisa, who provides a more elaborate demonstration of dancing to the rock 'n' roll music. Together with her brother Jimmy,

Figure 4.5 An introduction proper to rock 'n' roll from a variety of angles and perspectives

Figure 4.6 An introduction proper to rock 'n' roll from a variety of angles and perspectives

they embark on a heavily choreographed routine that draws on other kinds of dance as well as jitterbug, with a view to providing entertainment for the crowd (which has emptied the floor and made a circle around it in anticipation). At the same time, they are lowering down the levels of exuberance of the previous scene and contain any excess that may cause young people to misbehave (see Figure 4.7). This

Figure 4.7 A heavily choreographed routine continues to teach rock 'n' roll
dancing and contains any excess from an earlier scene that may
have led to unruly behaviour

explains why 'Rock-A-Beatin' Boogie' is edited at a much slower pace
than 'Alligator', consisting of just 16 shots over a duration of two
minutes and 15 seconds (for an 8.4 second ASL).

This performance is followed by another brief exchange between
Steve and Haley, with the former pitching the idea of managing the
band. This is where the fictional status of the real Haley becomes
known as he reveals himself to be a part time musician and full-time
tractor mechanic, with the rest of the band members being farmers and
only playing together on Saturday nights. Once again, this scene is
played for laughs as by that time the band was at the peak of its success and popularity and the idea that they were full time farmers and
mechanics (or had any other occupation) would have seemed ludicrous
to the young audiences. On the other hand, such a narrative choice
enables the possibility of the generic 'star-making' plot that will drive
the rest of the film and will give ample opportunities for diegetically
motivated performances that represent the film's main attraction. Perhaps more importantly, such a plot will be resolved by Haley's success,
of which the young audience of the film is fully aware and which they
can anticipate, giving the audience a climactic moment that the film
can build up as such. Finally, it provides Lisa with a second narrative
role next to that of the band dancer, the role of the amateur band's
spokesperson and manager, whose negotiations with Steve will not only
kick off the star-making process but will also instigate a romance plot
that is intricately linked with the main plot.

As is clear, by that time *Rock around the Clock*'s exploitation film cogs have been turning at full speed. Using the title of the most successful rock 'n' roll song as its title and featuring it on the opening credits, it explicitly imitated *Blackboard Jungle*, even though the comparisons with Richard Brooks's film stop there. This was sufficient, however, to solicit a similar response by some members of the audience who started dancing in the aisles, securing a 'lucrative association' with *Blackboard Jungle*. But that was only the beginning. After the use of the song kicked off the exploitation process, *Rock around the Clock* continued with borrowing exploitable elements associated with the band that made the song a hit, including building a fictional story around the band, while also using the rest of its songs, including a brand new one, as attractions with which it can punctuate the narrative and as pre-existing resources that can be economically reused.

Furthermore, the film's low budget and independent production (even under the umbrella of a major studio distributor) meant that the makers would not be able to make a straightforward biopic (as this would have meant extra funds to secure the rights of Haley and his band's story, shoot in particular locations, etc.). For this reason, as Hunter would put it, the filmmakers 'were constrained to play a different intertextual game' (Hunter 2009: 10), which in this case was a fictional story that plays on some elements associated with Haley (his country and western background), while focusing on a star-making scenario that would end with the band's success and rock 'n' roll's acceptance, a most topical issue for an exploitation film in early 1956. Indeed, the only aspect of the film that diverges from Hunter's approach is the fact that Katzman actually paid for the rights to use 'Rock around the Clock' and Bill Haley and His Comets, which makes their presence in the film 'legitimately purchased' (10) and therefore also raises questions of adaptation that we will discuss in the next section.

Once the star-making plot is set up – Steve decides to manage Bill Haley and His Comets with a view to using their music in order to make America dance again and in the process turn the amateur band into a professional outfit – *Rock around the Clock* switches gears and starts commenting on the nature of exploitation, becoming in the process an extremely self-reflexive text. This is primarily achieved through the narrative's emphasis on Steve's management and his actions to turn his plan into success or, to put it differently, his efforts to *exploit* a new cultural product in the entertainment industries with a view to both renewing a seemingly moribund part of US culture and benefitting financially. In doing this, the film throws the spotlight on to the rules of commercial exploitation and how they are enacted by various interested parties. And even though there had been many Hollywood films that focused on the entertainment industries, their operations and the machinations that take place behind the scenes, with Denisoff and Romanowski asserting that the 'bizzer discovering a band with a new sound' storyline was an 'old' and 'familiar' one (Denisoff and Romanowski 1990: 67), *RATC* lays down some of these operations with a degree of immediacy and clarity that is striking. It is as if master exploitation producer Sam Katzman gives lessons about how to engage in commercial exploitation.

The key way through which *RATC* reflects on the nature of exploitation is Steve's navigation of the politics of national booking agency Talbot Enterprises (run by Corinne Talbot, who is in love with him), the recruitment of disc jockey Alan Freed (also in a semi-fictional role) to help the band's success and the TV jamboree that provides the film with its triumphant ending. Each of these sections of the film provides a high degree of self-reflexivity as issues of commercial exploitation are placed at the forefront with their merits outlined or debated to a substantial extent. At the same time, the sections enable the diegetic inclusion of more songs, effectively acting as illustrations of successful exploitation strategies.

The first of these narrative threads revolves around Steve's professional and personal relationship with Talbot Enterprises and the ways in which it impacts on his management of the group. It is by far the most important and longest sequence of scenes in the film, especially as it also provides the context for a number of complications and problems that Steve will need to resolve, while also including a striking example of exploitation at work. As Steve has resisted the booking agency's owner and director Corinne Talbot's romantic advances, Talbot Enterprises is not interested in doing business with him. Although Corinne's refusal is motivated by sexual politics, once again, for the youth audience of the film such resistance would be understood more as the product of generational politics, that is, adult-led cultural institutions' inability to appreciate rock 'n' roll and its potential for commercial success.

Aiming at humiliating Steve who continues to resist her advances, Corinne decides to offer his clients a booking at an exclusive girls' school graduation prom. Bill Haley and His Comets would alternate with Tony Martinez and His Band, whose mix of cha-cha-cha, mambo and other Latino-infused music influences represents a much more appropriate choice for a pre-rock 'n' roll school dance, and therefore would all but guarantee the failure of Haley's music. However, yet again, for an audience watching the film *during* the rock 'n' roll era, Corinne's decision to book a rock 'n' roll band at a school dance would have been considered a surefire way to generate the kind of youth excitement that became synonymous with rock 'n' roll music, while it would also prove to be a savvy move from a business perspective. In this respect, although, in theory, Corinne's sexual politics motivation seems to go against her business acumen as the owner of the biggest booking agency in the US, in practice, her decision to book Bill Haley and His Comets in a prom enables her to make a hugely significant decision that provides another stepping stone for the national success of the band and its music. In the process, the film acknowledges the importance of the school pupils (read teenagers) as consumers of the subject of its exploitation. It may also be 'adapting' an episode of Bill Haley's pre-rock 'n' roll story, when as Bill Haley and the Saddlemen he and his band used to play gigs in high schools in Pennsylvania (Dawson 2005: 40).

Not surprisingly, Haley and his music set the prom on fire! Steve pitches again the band to Corinne, this time as a headline of a 'combo' that also includes Tony Martinez and His Band, Freddy Bell and the Bellboys, and Lisa and her brother. Corinne, who had been attending the graduation prom in order to see with her own eyes rock 'n' roll's failure, continues to resist and decides to use all her influence and business connections so that Haley and the band do not get any bookings. This motivates Alan Freed's introduction, whose voice on the radio prompts Corny to remember that Steve had helped him in the past by lending him money to organise a show in Texas. In real life, Freed was originally a Cleveland-based radio disc jockey who played R'n'B records before moving to New York and becoming a national celebrity. However, in *RATC*, Freed appears as a master of ceremonies in the fictional West River Club in New York City, while his past relationship with Steve is a convenient narrative contrition to motivate his appearance.

'You don't have to sell me on rock 'n' roll', Freed tells Steve, which prompts a fleeting smile on Steve's face. One can imagine the roar of the young audiences in hearing that line as by the time of the film's release Freed's reputation as a rock 'n' roll advocate had reached stratospheric heights. It is clear then that Freed's participation played a triple role in the film's project of exploiting a topical subject matter and a particular audience. Firstly, his mere presence legitimated the low-budget film while also acting as one of its main attractions. Secondly, his narrative presence, although playing a fictional version of himself, ensured a continuity with his real identity and brought distinct pleasures to the young viewers of the film who may also have been listening to his broadcasts or attending his dances. Finally, Freed's phenomenally popular shows worked in conjunction with the film in a very strong example of synergy even in the low-budget exploitation film sector.

The success of 'fictional' Bill Haley and His Comets after 'fictional' Alan Freed's intervention convinces Corinne Talbot to represent Steve's combo, provided that Lisa signs a contract that stipulates that she would not be marrying anyone for the duration of a three-year period, during which the agency's resources would be dedicated to promoting the band. Although this contract is once again motivated by Corinne's unabated interest in Steve, whose romance with Lisa continues to evolve, the narrative goes at great length to make it clear that this is also a sound business decision. In a striking scene between Corinne and Lisa, the former explains how exploitation works, especially when there is a sex element attached to it that can be used to entice young demographics:

> You are an investment, Lisa. You'll become an idol for teenagers. You'll develop a big public; hundreds of fan clubs; college boys would be voting you the girl they would most want to be caught in a compromising situation with. My agency will be spending a fortune on your publicity and exploitation. The bigger you or the boys [the band] become, the more money we all make. But you are the only girl of the outfit. The only one that means s-e-x. Like a movie star. I want my investment protected.

Fan clubs across the country; cultivation of an audience consisting of teenage boys and male college students; encouragement of that audience to consume the only female member of the band on the basis of sex; huge amounts of money dedicated to idol making activities; funds for publicity and exploitation – and that's just for a dancer associated with the band rather than the real article: the band and its music. But Talbot Enterprises (and Katzman and his crew) know that rock 'n' roll music and stardom need youth and sex appeal, which Bill Haley and His Comets did not possess. With Haley in his thirties and with the band propelled to superstardom having evolved from a background in country and western where sex appeal was not important, Lisa Johns represented the only avenue through which a seasoned national booking agency could play up the sex element – in a particularly gendered manner. This can be seen also in the film's use of actress Lisa Gaye in the scenes where she dances. She tends to be dressed in costumes that are revealing, as is the case in her dancing during the performance of 'R-O-C-K!' in which she is dressed in a black leotard and tights (see Figure 4.8) or, indeed, during the performance of the aforementioned 'Rock-A-Beatin' Boogie' in which the camera focuses on her moving posterior as she 'demonstrates' the dance with her brother. For David E. James, Lisa is not only essential to the film's narrative but also to its spectacle (James 2016: 41), which once again suggests that the film's exploitation tactics are well integrated in its narrative, making for a highly (and highly unusual) exploitation film.

The final element of the film's exploitation design is the television jamboree sequence that occupies approximately the last 15 minutes of the film. It consists of four consecutive performances introduced by Alan Freed, culminating with the third rendition of 'Rock around the Clock' in the film, which takes us to the closing credits. In many ways, it is a predictable narrative tactic: end the film with its key attraction, three bands performing songs in what is a climax of energy and joy, with the songs following each other in quick succession and with the narrative only interrupting them for brief periods to tidy up any loose ends. Furthermore, the rendition of 'Rock around the Clock' is the only time when audiences see Bill Haley and His Comets perform its smash hit, with the other two consisting of the song playing over the opening credits and later as part of a montage sequence. It would have been a major disappointment for the young audience if they watched a

Figure 4.8 S-E-X! Rock 'n' roll needs youth and sex appeal, and Lisa Johns has both as she becomes the focal point of Talbot Enterprises' exploitation strategy

film entitled *Rock around the Clock* but without a performance of the title song.

However, yet again, the film goes beyond the actual presentation of the jamboree and provides significant information about its rationale and its organisation. As soon as it becomes clear that Bill Haley and His Comets, with the support of Talbot Enterprises, have been successful nationwide, Steve pitches the idea of the jamboree to Corinne, who accepts it with enthusiasm. This is because Steve has thought of all the details, including holding the event in Los Angeles, the capital of the entertainment industry; organising its recording and broadcast for the beginning of July to ensure that 'kids [will be] out of school', which will maximise business for his clients; and convincing one of the major networks to televise the event to ensure national coverage via the network's affiliates. Alan Freed would be the master of ceremonies, not only because his name is synonymous with rock 'n' roll but because he has had strong experience in both broadcasting and live events.

Given this attention to detail, it is not surprising that Steve's jamboree is a great success, while between performances, in a nice fell swoop, Lisa resolves both the main plotline by acknowledging Steve's management skills in bringing rock 'n' roll to the nation (answering the narrative's opening question of whether Steve is a good manager) and the romance plotline by revealing that she has been married to him. Meanwhile Steve in New York explains to Corinne that the marriage took place before the contract Lisa signed and therefore there could be no legal repercussions (even though it is unclear how significant the financial repercussions would be given that the sex appeal of the band is now officially 'off the market'). Finally, the very last shot is back in Los Angeles with all the kids dancing to 'Rock around the Clock', resolving the final narrative question of whether Steve can make America dance again.

With the film outlining the rules of exploitation with such clarity and in such detail, it is not surprising that the rock 'n' roll films that followed took pages from Katzman's playbook. Taking only *Shake, Rattle and Rock!* and *Rock, Rock, Rock!* as examples, one can see Alan Freed playing again a version of himself, Lisa Gaye cast again as the female romantic lead, televised jamborees or jamboree-like events presenting songs in succession, dancing scenes of exuberant jitterbugging, emphasis on the sex appeal of the female teen, interaction of young people with the stars and even end credit tag lines that responded to *Rock around the Clock*'s 'The Living End'. Perhaps the ultimate imitation of *RATC* was *Twist Around the Clock* (Rudolph, 1961). Produced by Sam Katzman with a view to exploit the twist craze and

Chubby Checker's success, the film is an almost identical remake of *RATC* scene for scene.

The Art of Adaptation

If the main motivation for any film adaptation is 'the marketing aura of the original', then few source texts in the mid-1950s could claim a stronger aura than the song 'Rock around the Clock'. By the time the film was announced in the trade press (November 1955) the song's sales in the US were close to 2 million discs, with *Variety* predicting that it was on course to surpass 'Tennessee Waltz', the biggest-selling record of the first half of the decade ('"Tennessee Waltz" Steps Out ...' 1951: 42). And then, of course, was the band behind the song, who was riding a wave of phenomenal commercial success between 1955 and 1957, in the US and internationally. Indeed, in September 1956, Bill Haley and His Comets had no fewer than five songs in the UK's NME Top 20 simultaneously ('Best Selling ...' 1956: 66), while by early 1957 'Rock around the Clock' became the first record to sell more than 1 million records in the UK ('Haley "Rock" ...' 1957: 51).

Having secured both the rights to use the song's title as the title of the film and the services of the band that popularised it at the peak of their success as actors/performers, together with those of Alan Freed who helped popularise the music under the label 'rock 'n' roll', it is clear that there were many avenues for Katzman and his team to take in crafting *RATC*. As we argue below, Katzman used a number of sources for the film, avoiding overreliance on a single prior text such as the song or the band's biography. Specifically, Katzman chose to adapt a chapter of the *history* of rock 'n' roll by using the rise of Bill Haley and His Comets to success as a focal point. However, the story of Haley and his band is neither factually accurate nor represented as a biopic, despite the fact that Bill Haley and His Comets appear under their real names. Rather, the band is used as the main thread in a narrative about making America dance again at a time when swing seemed to have had its course and people were more interested in jazz and other sounds rather than dancing. In this respect, rock 'n' roll is represented as having a particular purpose and role in the broader history of popular music, dancing and the United States, which explains the adaptation tactics of Katzman and his team: they took 'marketing possibilities that the prior text[s] generate[d] and used them to serve different purposes and reach audiences in the new medium in different ways' (Leitch 2009: 261).

Of course, the key issue with the film's take on the history of rock 'n' roll was the complete erasure of the other streams of music that influenced its emergence, especially rhythm and blues. R'n'B had emerged in the 1950s as a commercially successful category of music drawing on blues, gospel and other types of music associated with African American culture, forcing the disappearance of the term 'race music' (James 2016: 2) and promising a more integrated popular music landscape. However, this musical amalgamation brought a very real integration of White and African American populations, especially young people, at a time when the US was still segregated (with school desegregation becoming law only in 1954, the year of the first record-ing of 'Rock around the Clock' by Bill Haley and His Comets). This resulted in a huge outcry, especially as 'rhythm and blues, with its emphasis on the backbeat and the frequent use of licentious lyrics, was "perceived [by the White, adult population] as being overtly sexual in both lyrics and performance – and this bordered on immorality"' (Klein 2011: 114). Taken together with its association with juvenile delinquency it was clear that the screen representation of rock 'n' roll was a minefield for commercially focused film producers.

This perhaps explains the filmmakers' decision to erase rhythm and blues' connection to rock 'n' roll and focus almost exclusively on its relationship to country and western, through the story of Bill Haley and His Comets. Country and western had also emerged from earlier forms of music, mostly associated with hillbilly and folk music, espe-cially when the addition of electric guitars shifted the music from a 'folk orientation' to honky-tonk and roadhouse entertainment (Medo-voi 2005: 106). However, at the same time, country 'absorbed more elements of black music than were accepted into the mainstream pop of the time' (Gillett 1996: 8), while Southern rockabilly musicians like Jerry Lee Lewis, who, as Simon Frith points out, added 'a black drive to hillbilly sounds' (Frith 1983: 26), became instrumental in making rock 'n' roll acceptable to White people in the recently desegregated South.

However, the filmmakers made one concession on that front by including two performances by The Platters, 'the only authentic rhythm and blues act to reach the top 10 in 1955' (Denisoff and Romanowski 1990: 68). Although their performances of 'Only You' and 'The Great Pretender' are the least integrated narratively of all performances in *RATC*, for John Mundy, their presence alone in a film together with White artists was of particular significance (Mundy 1999: 108), paving the way for other rock 'n' roll films to incorporate more Black artists. For James, on the other hand, any association of the group with rock 'n' roll 'is stripped of any identification with urban crowds and blacks', with the film only recognising the hillbilly origin of rock 'n' roll (James 2016: 35); disagreement between scholars on this point demonstrates the difficulty for film producers in navigating the racial politics of the time.

Similarly, as we argued in Chapter 1, the film all but erases any associations between rock 'n' roll and juvenile delinquency. With a lot of the early scenes taking place in a small town, any narrative opportunities for delinquency (which is much more easily associated with big cities and urban centres) are thwarted. The young people are out, going to a dance on Saturday night, but there is no trouble, with the dance fully approved by the older generation of Strawberry Springs. The only occasion where there is a narrative opportunity for delinquency is during the graduation prom at the exclusive girls' school in Connecticut. But, as we also argued in Chapter 1, the confrontation between a dancing couple and the two conservative female teachers is played for comedy and represents an example of the couple's cultural rebellion rather than an expression of delinquency.

As is evident, the marketing possibilities generated by the prior texts do serve different purposes in the medium of film and, indeed, reach its audiences in different ways, as Leitch argues. Aiming to provide an entertaining history of rock 'n' roll, *Rock around the Clock* zeroes in on the most visible White band of that time and its most recognisable and successful song as shorthand for that history, while also closing down other possible narrative avenues that could complicate this process and jeopardise the film's commercial success. In doing this, *Rock around the Clock* adheres to almost all the elements of postliterary adaptation as identified by Leitch. For instance, one can certainly see the 'playful pleasures' provided by the 'ingenuity with which features of the prior text have been preserved in the new medium' (Leitch 2009: 261), whether it is Haley and his band members' country and western background or the fact that 'Rock around the Clock' becomes the song with which they are trying to break into the national music market or even the fact that one of the dancers in Strawberry Springs exclaims 'crazy, man, crazy' when asked about her dancing routine – which is the title of a 1953 song by Bill Haley and His Comets. One can also easily detect the 'activation of narrative potentialities' (262) implicit in the history of the band, the time it took for 'Rock around the Clock' to be successful, the role Alan Freed played in the popularisaton of rock 'n' roll, and others.

The makers of the film also used 'circumstantial detail by evoking resonant historical settings' (Leitch 2009: 262), with the alleged decline of swing and big band music used masterfully to motivate the emergence of rock 'n' roll and its acknowledgement as a non-threatening next step in popular dance music. They also drew on 'earlier narrative texts and utiliz[ed] genre conventions' (ibid.) in order to ensure that the film would remain 'familiar' even though it had on its shoulders the burden of representing a new cultural phenomenon. Specifically, they drew on music biopics and their conventions of staging multiple performances within a narrative about the long road to success, with *The Glenn Miller Story* and *The Benny Goodman Story* being such examples. They also drew on backstage musicals and their convention of featuring a dual focus narrative with a romance story between a man and a woman intersecting with a production of a show and the challenges this presents, with films such as *Footlight Parade* (Bacon, 1933) and *White Christmas* (Curtiz, 1953) providing interesting examples.

Furthermore, Katzman and his team also drew from films featuring jitterbug dancing, especially *Running Wild* (Biberman, 1955), which featured Bill Haley and His Comets' song 'Razzle Dazzle' (played in a jukebox) and which contains probably the earliest example of rock 'n' roll dancing in a non-musical film. The key male dancer in *Running Wild*, Lou Southern, also appeared in *The Benny Goodman Story* as a jitterbug dancer before becoming the dancer through which Steve and Corny are introduced to rock 'n' roll at the Strawberry Springs dance (see Figure 4.6 above). Given all this eclectic mix of influences and inspirations, including its playful ending with the phrase 'The Living End' as 'Rock around the Clock' still plays on the credits, it is not surprising that the film also adheres to Leitch's final characteristic of postliterary adaptations: 'generally and often incongruously lightsome tone suggesting that this sort of adaptation is fundamentally more whimsical than the serious adaptation of novels or plays or stories' (Leitch 2009: 262).

If *Rock around the Clock* is a perfect example of postliterary adaptation as it was defined by Leitch, it also seems to draw on several of the modes of adapting a song into film as identified by Inglis. Although Haley's and Freed's appearance in the film is not driven by any desire to legitimate them as actors, it is nonetheless the case that *RATC* follows a well-established Hollywood tradition of using musicians playing versions of themselves and using their real names in supporting roles (see, for instance, Benny Goodman in *The Gang's All Here* [Berkeley, 1943], Louis Armstrong in *High Society* [Walters, 1956] and Artie Shaw in *Dancing Co-Ed* [Simon, 1939]). This practice, however, sometimes hides the fact that some of these films *are* about the music associated with these musicians, which provides 'the main context' for the film, and that the appearance of these musicians as actors in a supporting role is the icing on a cake, the main ingredient for which is their music. Understood in this way, it is clear that *Rock around the Clock is* about Bill Haley's rock 'n' roll, with his music providing the main context for the film.

Rock around the Clock features nine songs by Bill Haley and His Comets, two by The Platters, four by Tony Martinez and His Band and two by Freddie Bell and the Bellboys. Out of these 17 songs, only one, 'See You Later, Alligator' was a new song that had been released just prior to the film's opening. This suggests that *RATC* is also a film 'where the score is driven by pre-existing tracks', recorded way before the film was conceptualised and produced. While Inglis uses this category to characterise more recent films such as *American Graffiti* (Lucas, 1973) and *The Big Chill* (Kasdan, 1983) that use classic hits and trade in the business of nostalgia, one could use this category more literally and see it as another innovative aspect of *RATC* given the ways it trades in the very recent past and present of rock 'n' roll.

Where the issue becomes more complicated is when considering the proposition of whether (and how) the film adapts music. Inglis here seems to limit his discussion to films borrowing a song title and providing 'often little acknowledgement of the song's presence other than use as incidental background music'. Here one could also think of various motifs based on the main song or theme in a film that are repeated as incidental music throughout a film. However, *Rock around the Clock* does much more than that. From the use of the song in the credits and its invitation to the young audience to break with spectatorship decorum and dance in the aisles, to its selection as the band's representative work in an effort to be successful and to establish rock 'n' roll as a dance music, to its play over the final credit as evidence of success and acceptance, 'Rock around the Clock' certainly gives more to the film than a title and a main tune. And even though we do not want to go as far as James, who argued that it is the 'itinerary' of the song, 'from small independent forms of production to the cultural center' (James 2016: 42), that is at the core of the film, and suggest instead that it metonymically stands for rock 'n' roll, we do agree with him that *RATC* 'appropriated Haley's song' and 'turned [it] into a film' (33).

We would like to close this chapter with a comment about the film's status as a biopic and return to Inglis's three answers to the question of what biopics 'seek to do'. As we already noted, *RATC* may be the one film that sits comfortably within the genre without being a straightforward biopic, while arguably also doing all three of the things that biopics seek to do: present a plausible account of historical events; fabricate a version of history; and fashion a commercially appealing product in which accuracy may be seen as irrelevant. Although the film is furthest removed from the first objective and is much better represented by the second and certainly by the third one, what becomes important here, again, is to understand this from the perspective of its audience. With *RATC* marketed specifically to teenagers who love rock 'n' roll music, one wonders about the extent to which the events narrated were *perceived* by that audience as 'a more or less plausible account of historical events' or as 'a version of history that may be subjective, idiosyncratic, prejudiced'. Would 13-year-old kids be able to ascertain if the story of rock 'n' roll via Bill Haley and His Comets presented to them is inaccurate, in the same way, perhaps, that Benny Goodman and Glenn Miller adult fans would be able to when it came to assessing the two musicians' respective biopics? Would some young audience members be able to make such an assertion depending on their race? Would audiences outside the US (where the film was an even bigger commercial success) be able to make this distinction?

It is impossible to provide empirically grounded answers to these questions. We would like, however, to suggest that even if one takes *Rock around the Clock* as a biopic that provides a highly selective, subjective, idiosyncratic and prejudiced version of real events in which Bill Hayley and His Comets played a small but very visible role, its core audience would not be equipped or willing to assess, nor interested in assessing, its historical accuracy. Perhaps older teenagers and young adults who had been following the rapid developments of rock 'n' roll in the mid-1950s and who have been accessing information through other media like magazines and newspapers may have been in a position to make such an assessment. However, even in this case, there is no guarantee that the White-dominated mainstream media would provide a more accurate story. In this sense, *Rock around the Clock could* pass as a film that provided a more or less plausible account of very specific historical events as the 'whole story'. Or, to put it differently, *Rock Around the Clock* 'engage[d] in a dialogue with known information about the titular song and its most famous performer' (Reinsch 2013: 17) and used that part to stand for the whole.

Taking all the above into consideration, it makes more sense to side with Inglis's third answer: 'fashion a commercially attractive product in which questions of accuracy and evidence are actually seen as irrelevant' (but replace 'are actually' with 'can be' to account for the fact that one cannot provide an empirically grounded answer to this question). This means acknowledging that the film was not made for 'historical accuracy and literal truth' but for entertainment and commercial success and that factors such as studio style, stardom and genre convention have been important in shaping it. This brings us full circle to Sam Katzman and his exploitative production practices that we examined in the previous chapters. Given his explicitly stated focus on cashing in on fads, fashions and topical subject matter, and especially the way he handled the corrupt city officials film cycle that preceded his music teenpics, one can argue that historical accuracy was not an objective for *Rock around the Clock*, as it was not an issue for its teenage audience.

Conclusion

This chapter continued to build on work that sees *Rock around the Clock* as an aesthetically complex film, the product of exploitation film practices and film adaptation modes that combine to create a film that is both extremely self-reflexive and difficult to categorise. Its exploitation practices are wide ranging and involve borrowing from a number of other films to create a narrative that is about the exploitation of a new kind of music and provides a series of opportunities for the film to outline how exploitation works and comment on its working. Every step of the way, the film is aware of the audience it targets, privileging a style that provides easy access to the narrative and including scenes that indulge the young audiences. On the other hand, its approach to adaptation is highly eclectic and demonstrates the complex ways in which it uses the song 'Rock around the Clock', the biography of Bill Haley and His Comets, and influences from different types and genres of film. The result is a highly original postliterary adaptation of a type of music and song that playfully also includes certain historical facts, to the extent that the film can also pass for a biopic, despite the distorted version of historical events that attaches itself to. Although such an approach runs the danger of making the film not credible, its focus on a teen audience who is not expected to or is not equipped to deal with such issues makes this a moot point and the film's phenomenal box-office success certainly justified the practices used to make it.

Note

1 'Let's Fall in Love' had been a major success for bandleader-pianist Eddy Duchin, whose life was dramatized in Columbia's biggest commercial success in 1956, *The Eddy Duchin Story* (Sidney).

Coda
The Living End

The increasing canonisation of *Rock around the Clock* in recent decades by scholars and other critics, who have demonstrated the sophistication and complexity that permeates this lowly exploitation film and to which this book contributes, does not negate the fact that the film has been all but forgotten by popular culture. Its exploitation of the emergence of rock 'n' roll in the mid-1950s, especially of the staggering commercial success of Bill Haley and His Comets, whose songs sold millions of copies and dominated the charts in the US and internationally in the 1955–57 period, helped the film record a lengthy presence in theatres worldwide that was rare for a low-budget exploitation picture. Released in March 1956, *RATC* played throughout the year in US theatres, with newspapers occasionally reporting on the 'troubles' made by young cinema patrons during or after the film, as we noted earlier in this book.

The film received a major boost from its UK release on 27 August 1956, in a wave of more (and more substantial) reports about youth riots and as Bill Haley and His Comets enjoyed a similar level of success in that country. As a matter of fact, *RATC* continued to play internationally well into 1957, with the *Hollywood Reporter* stating that by August of that year, 18 months into its release, it had recorded a $4 million worldwide box-office gross ('$4 Million Already' 1957: 1) and that it had helped Columbia increase its profits internationally by 24% compared to the previous year ('Columbia Foreign Business' 1957: 17). By the end of 1957, however, the film had disappeared from the theatres, with only the occasional reissue in the first half of the 1960s, usually as a double bill with Katzman's *Twist around the Clock* (Randolph, 1961) ('The Exhibitor Has ...' 1962: B6) and *Don't Knock the Twist* (Randolph, 1962) ('The Exhibitor Has ...' 1965: A4).

In 1966, *RATC* was one of 60 titles selected by its distributor for its 'Columbia Group II Post-1950' package of films to sell to local

DOI: 10.4324/9781315544908-6

television stations. With the package consisting of 10 'highlighters' and 13 star-led productions, *RATC* appears on the list of the remaining 37 films, alongside other Katzman-produced titles, firmly identified as cheap programming for local broadcasters ('Screen Gems Brochure ...' 1966: 7). The film's inclusion in the package may have been influenced by a 'revival' of Haley's music, especially 'Rock around the Clock', which by 1964 had sold an estimated 15 million copies and was considered a '"done" disc' (Nicholl 1964: 11). With his career in decline since 1958, and amid legal issues relating to tax evasion, Haley and his band had disappeared from the limelight as spectacularly as they had found fame only three years prior.

Haley's revival did not take place as expected. However, in 1973, a documentary celebrating the rock 'n' roll pioneers under the title *Let the Good Times Roll* (Abel and Levin), as well as George Lucas's *American Graffiti*, gave Haley, his signature song and even Katzman's film a new lease of life. The former included recorded performances of rock 'n' roll's biggest names as they toured the country in packaged shows under the 'Rock and Roll Revival' banner, interspersed with archival footage of the artists and bands in their prime, interviews as well as other footage about rock 'n' roll in the 1950s. Bill Haley and His Comets appear early in the film performing 'Rock around the Clock' and 'Shake, Rattle and Roll', with the performance of the former edited in a split screen with footage from *Blackboard Jungle* and *RATC* as well as *The Wild One* and *I Was a Teenage Werewolf* (Fowler Jr., 1957). The scenes from *RATC* last only a few seconds and include shots of young people dancing and of the montage sequence showing the emergence of rock 'n' roll. As for Haley and the band, well into their forties in 1973, they look rather out of place, especially when compared to Little Richard and Chuck Berry, who give hugely energetic performances. However, the fact that the performance of 'Rock around the Clock' is juxtaposed with scenes from 1950s youth films for the duration of the song highlights strongly its significance for American cinema and the youth cultures it represented in that era (with no other performance in the film enjoying such a connection).

American Graffiti, on the other hand, kicked off a wave of nostalgia for 'the US fifties', not necessarily the decade itself, but the idea of a set period that also includes the early 1960s as one of innocence, fun and optimism. Dominated by baby boom youth, mobility and consumption, this 'golden era' inevitably came to a crushing end as social, political and economic developments in the US and internationally (the nuclear race, the Vietnam War, etc.) established a climate of uncertainty. 'Rock around the Clock' is heard over the opening credits of this film too, which includes a wall-to-wall soundtrack of rock 'n' roll titles from the 1950s, such as 'Ain't that a Shame' (by Fats Domino), 'The Great Pretender' (The Platters) and 'Chantilly Lace' (The Big Popper) as well as hits from the early 1960s such as 'Runaway' (Del Shannon). This time, however, there were no reports of audience disturbances or dancing in the aisles. Instead, there were debates about the extent to which *American Graffiti* used rock 'n' roll as part of a well-calculated exercise in nostalgia, a 'commodified nostalgia', that made the film a runaway success at the box office and influenced other films such as *The Big Chill* (Kasdan, 1983) (Shumway 1999: 39, 43–4).

Although these films highlighted primarily the importance of the song rather than Katzman's film, the latter started to exert its influence in popular culture in more surreptitious ways, especially in the 1980s. That decade became synonymous with a (new) golden age of youth cinema as films that focused on the experience of teenagers and other young people proved both significant box-office hits and staked a strong claim in defining the era culturally. These films were powered by the spectacular success of MTV (established in 1981), which provided both marketing opportunities and a new aesthetic as exemplified by the pop video. They were also endorsed by the increasingly synergistic efforts of the major studios, which were pushing in the marketplace both their films and tie-in soundtracks made by record labels that were often subsidiaries of the same conglomerate. It is not surprising then that youth films of the 1980s were often music-led, which invited scholars to compare them to MTV's fast-edited videos (see Prince 2002: 308–9).

Footloose (Ross, 1984), a major box-office hit for Paramount, is a key film that was influenced by *RATC* (although it also has several elements in common with films such as *Don't Knock the Rock* and *Shake, Rattle and Rock!* that adopt a put-rock-'n'-roll-on-trial narrative). Its story focuses on high school boy Ren, who moves with his mother from Chicago, IL to Beaumont, NC only to find an environment more akin to the 1950s than the early 1980s. The town authorities have passed laws that banned rock music and dancing because of an accident that caused the death of several young people after a party. Feeling that such a decision denies the right of young people to be young, Ren spearheads an effort to convince the authorities to allow a school dance to take place so that he and his friends are able to celebrate their youth. The film's emphasis on dancing and its acceptance by the establishment is a shorthand for the acceptance of a music that represents a youth culture that cannot be suppressed. The authorities initially resist Ren's proposal but then they find themselves trying to suppress other forms of culture (burning 'dangerous' books), which prompts the town pastor to reconsider his view and convince the authorities to give their permission. The dance takes place, but under the auspices of a high school prom that also involves a lot of manual labour by the students to transform an old warehouse into a suitable space. In doing this, *Footloose* ensures that the music and dancing take place within a heavily institutionalised (and safe) context and away from the unmonitored (and dangerous) saloons, which the youngsters had secretly used as the only alternative outside the town. As for the law banning music and dancing, it is not clear if it would be revoked after the dance.

But it is another landmark youth film of the 1980s that is, arguably, closest to *RATC*: *Dirty Dancing* (Ardolino, 1987). The film was produced outside the studios by Vestron, a video company that in 1986 branched out to film production to ensure a flow of content for its booming videocassette release business. Vestron conceptualised *Dirty Dancing* as a low-budget film with young stars and a director with little experience in film but with credits in dance documentaries for television. Besides its humble origins, the production also seems to have updated the exploitation film model for the 1980s, with its star Jennifer Grey admitting in an interview that it was not clear to her during the production if the movie would be 'really dirty' and whether she would be a 'pawn in this kind of weird softcore porn movie'.[1]

It is at the level of narrative, however, that *Dirty Dancing* has an even stronger affinity with *RATC*. Although its story takes place in 1963, the heroine's voiceover narration situates it clearly in the 'long 50s', a time before The Beatles and before the Kennedy assassination. A teenage girl goes for a family vacation in a mountain resort only to see her sexual desire awakened by an older male resort dancer who teaches her how to dance 'dirty'. 'Dirty' here refers to a sensual form of dancing that in a mainstream, White, 1950s environment would seem inappropriate, especially as the music for it tends to be Black or Latino in origin. Cue to another wall-to-wall soundtrack that provides many opportunities for dirty dancing, with two of the songs ('Love Is Strange' and 'In the Still of the Night') released in 1956, the year of *RATC*, and many other songs released contemporaneously and even after the time when the narrative takes place.

However, in making young, middle-class, Jewish 'Baby' Houseman learn to 'dirty dance' as a way of making acceptable to the mainstream culture that comes from other classes, races and ethnicities at the time when America was about to move from the 'fifties' to the 'sixties',

Dirty Dancing also engages in the same politics of whitewashing that characterised *RATC*. Despite the Black and Latino origin of most of the music, the dirty dancers in the film are all White (bar two couples that appear for a few seconds in the background of shots) and claim that they learnt the dancing 'back home' where 'the kids were doing it' (without explaining where the 'home' is and who the 'kids' were). Furthermore, the anachronistic soundtrack does not only include songs by Black artists such as Otis Redding that were released after the film's narrative time but also songs by White artists of the 1980s, a strategy that distorts further the origins of the music and dance in the film, while at the same time making them 'contemporary' for its target audience. Neither interested in realistic audiovisual representation nor on historical accuracy (McNelis 2013: 240), *Dirty Dancing* presents the acceptance of a potentially disruptive and sexually threatening new youth culture in a way that is also easily recuperated by the neo-conservative mainstream of Reagan's America as was the case with the 1950s rock 'n' roll in *RATC*.

But perhaps the most obvious influence of *RATC* in popular culture came two years after *Dirty Dancing* (in June 1989) and in the form of the song 'Swing the Mood' by Jive Bunny and the Mastermixers. Released at the peak of a trend that saw songs sampling older songs, 'Swing the Mood' consisted almost entirely of sampled extracts from songs by rock 'n' roll pioneers such as Little Richard, Elvis Presley and The Everly Brothers, bookmarked by Glenn Miller's 'In the Mood'. At the start of the song, as soon as the 48-second sampling of 'In the Mood' ends, a 27-second section of 'Rock around the Clock' follows. In one fell swoop, the song's creators move from one of swing's best-known instrumentals to one of rock 'n' roll's best-known songs, demonstrating anew the continuum within which popular music circulates and the fact that it is (or should be) made primarily for dancing by young people. Derided upon its release by critics, 'Swing the Mood' became a huge success in the charts worldwide, spawning further similarly produced singles and later *Jive Bunny: The Album* (1989). Had he been able to see not only his approach to exploitation but also the narrative premise of *RATC* being imitated 33 years later, Sam Katzman would have definitely approved.

Note

1 Grey's interview is included in the special features of the film's 20th anniversary DVD release (Region 2). It is also available on YouTube (www.you tube.com/watch?v=grgv5nRL7D0).

Bibliography

'A Rock 'n' Roll Feature' (1955) *Variety*, 23 November, p. 4.

Ackerman, P. (1955) 'Tin Pan Alley Fade on Pop Music Broader Horizons', *Billboard*, 15 October, pp. 1, 16.

Altschuler, G.C. (2003) *All Shook Up: How Rock 'n' Roll Changed America*, New York, NY: Oxford University Press.

'"Anchors Aweigh" Being Reissued' (1955) *Hollywood Reporter*, 26 January, p. 4.

Arneel, G. (1957) '109 Top Money Films of 1956', *Variety*, 2 January, p. 4.

Arneel, G. (1956) 'America's 107 Million-$ Films', *Variety*, 25 January, pp. 1, 15.

Baker, D. (2013) 'Elvis Goes to Hollywood: Authenticity, Resistance, Commodification and the Mainstream', in S. Baker, A. Bennett and J. Taylor (eds) *Redefining Mainstream Popular Music*, London: Routledge, pp. 89–101.

Balio, T. (2018) *MGM*, London: Routledge.

Balio, T. (1995) *Grand Design: Hollywood as a Modern Business Enterprise, 1930–1939*, Berkeley, CA: University of California Press.

Balio, T. (1976) *United Artists: The Company Built by the Stars*, Madison, WI: University of Wisconsin Press.

Barber, R. (1962) 'The Seven Days of Sam Katzman', *Show*, June, pp. 98–101.

'Best Selling Pop Records in Britain' (1956) *Billboard*, 6 October, p. 66.

Betrock, A. (1986) *The I Was a Teenage Juvenile Delinquent Rock 'n' Roll Horror Beach Party Movie Book: A Complete Guide to the Teen Exploitation Film, 1954–1969*, New York, NY: St. Martin's Press.

'Blackboard Jungle' (n.d.) American Film Institute Catalogue, online, https://catalog.afi.com/Catalog/moviedetails/53472.

'"Blackboard Jungle" Acquired by MGM' (1954) *Hollywood Reporter*, 13 April, p. 1.

Blottner, G. (2015) *Columbia Noir: Complete Filmography, 1940–1962*, Jefferson, NC: McFarland Publishing.

Brake, M. (1985) *Comparative Youth Culture: The Sociology of Youth Culture and Youth Subcultures in America, Britain and Canada*, London: Routledge and Kegan Paul.

Brickman, B.J. (2014) *New American Teenagers: The Lost Generation of Youth in 1970s Film*, New York, NY: Bloomsbury Academic.

Brode, D. (2015) *Sex, Drugs & Rock 'n' Roll: The Evolution of an American Youth Culture*, New York, NY: Peter Lang.

Brog. (1956) '"Rock, Rock, Rock!"', *Variety*, 16 December, p. 6.

Brog. (1955) '"Running Wild"', *Variety*, 2 November, p. 6.

Bundy, J. (1956) 'Freed's New Movie Adds up to Triple Threat $'s', *Billboard*, 17 November, pp. 16, 30.

Bundy, J. (1955) 'D.J.'s Men of Varied Interests, Most of Which Involve Loot', *Billboard*, 31 December, pp. 11–12.

'Chart Comments' (1955) *Billboard*, 14 May, p. 30.

Chute, D. (1986) 'That's Exploitation! Wages of Sin', *Film Comment*, Vol. 22, No. 4, July–August, pp. 32–48.

'Col Finds Rowdy Reports Kick Back at "Rock" Pic' (1956) *Variety*, 11 April, p. 60.

'Columbia Foreign Business 24 percent above Year Ago' (1957) *Hollywood Reporter*, 18 March, pp. 1, 17.

'Congress Investigates: The Senate Judiciary Committee's Subcommittee on Juvenile Delinquency Investigates Comic Books in the 1950s' (n.d.) National Archives, online, www.archives.gov/legislative/resources/education/comic-books.

Davis, B. (2012) *The Battle for the Bs: 1950s Hollywood and the Rebirth of Low-Budget Cinema*, New Brunswick, NJ: Rutgers University Press.

Davis, R.L. (1997) *Celluloid Mirrors: Hollywood and American Society since 1945*, London: Harcourt Brace College Publishers.

Dawson, J. (2005) *Rock around the Clock: The Record that Started the Rock Revolution*, San Franciso, CA: Backbeat Books.

Dawson, J. and Propes, S. (1992) *What Was the First Rock 'n' Roll Record?* London: Faber and Faber.

'Delinquency Theme Hot, M-G Speeding Release of Jungle' (1955) *Variety*, 26 January, p. 7.

Dellar, F. (2019) 'What Was the First Rock Soundtrack Album?', *Mojo*, No. 312, November, p. 126.

Denisoff, S. and Romanowski, W. (1990) 'Katzman's "Rock around the Clock": A Pseudo-historic Event', *Journal of Popular Culture*, Vol. 24, No. 1, pp. 65–78.

Dixon, W.W. (2005) *Lost in the Fifties: Recovering Phantom Hollywood*, Carbondale, IL: South Illinois University Press.

Doherty, T. (2002) *Teenagers and Teenpics: The Juvenilization of American Movies in the 1950s*, Revised and Expanded Edition, Philadelphia, PA: Temple University Press.

Doherty, T. (1995) 'Teenagers and Teenpics, 1955–1957: A Study of Exploitation Filmmaking', in J. Staiger (ed) *The Studio System*, New Brunswick, NJ: Rutgers University Press, pp. 298–316.

Doherty, T. (1988) *Teenagers and Teenpics: The Juvenilization of American Movies in the 1950s*, Boston, MA: Unwin Hyman.

Driscoll, C. (2011) *Teen Film: A Critical Introduction*, New York, NY: Berg.

'Fats Domino Signed' (1956) *Hollywood Reporter*, 31 July, p. 8.

Finler, J.W. (2003) *The Hollywood Story*, 3rd Edition, London: Wallflower Press.

Flynn, C. and McCarthy, T. (1975) 'The Economic Imperative: Why Was the B Movie Necessary?', in T. McCarthy and C. Flynn (eds) *King of the Bs: Working within the Hollywood System*, New York, NY: E.P. Dutton and Co., pp. 13–47.

'$4 Million Already Crossed by $250,000 Katzman Pic' (1957) *Hollywood Reporter*, 22 August, p. 1.

Frith, S. (1983) *Sound Effects: Youth, Leisure and the Politics of Rock 'n' Roll*, London: Constable.

Gilbert, J. (1986) *A Cycle of Outrage: America's Reaction to the Juvenile Delinquent in the 1950s*, New York, NY: Oxford University Press.

Gillett, C. (1996) *The Sound of the City: The Rise of Rock & Roll*, 3rd Edition, London: Souvenir Press.

'"Gimmick" Sub for "Formula"' (1955) *Variety*, 1 June, pp. 4, 22.

Gioia, T. (1998) *The History of Jazz*, New York, NY: Oxford University Press.

Gomery, D. (1986) *The Hollywood Studio System*, New York, NY: St. Martin's Press.

Gordon, A. (1984) 'The Pit and the Pen: History of AIP Terror, Part VIII – Corman Time Travels and Alex Rocks', *Fangoria*, No. 34, March, pp. 29–31.

Grant, B.K. (1986) 'The Classic Hollywood Musical and the "Problem" of Rock 'n' Roll', *Journal of Popular Film and Television*, Vol. 13, No. 4, pp. 195–205.

Green, A. (1954) 'Show Biz 1953 – Wotta Year', *Variety*, 6 January, pp. 1, 58–9.

Haley, B. (1957) 'Bill Haley Writes', *New Musical Express*, 4 January, p. 9.

'Haley and Comets Switch Managers' (1954) *Variety*, 17 July, p. 58.

'Haley "Rock" Disk Hits 1,000,000 in U.K. Sales' (1957) *Variety*, 6 February, p. 51.

'Haley's "Clock" Disk Nears 2,000,000 Mark' (1955) *Variety*, 30 November, p. 1.

Hammer, A.R. (1957) 'Fad also Rocks Cash Registers', *New York Times*, 23 February, p. 12.

Hanke, K. (1995) 'Sam Katzman', in J. McCarty (ed) *The Sleaze Merchants: Adventures in Exploitation Filmmaking*, New York, NY: St Martin's Press, pp. 3–16.

Hoberman, J. (2014) 'When Senator Kefauver Inspired the Scripts', *New York Times*, 16 February, pp. R11, R21.

Hunter, I.Q. (2009) 'Exploitation as Adaptation', in I.R. Smith (ed) *Cultural Borrowings: Appropriation, Reworking, Transformation*, Vol. 15, Scope: An Online Journal of Film and Television Studies, Nottingham, pp. 8–32, www.nottingham.ac.uk/scope/documents/2009/culturalborrowingsebook.pdf.

'Independent Activity Holds Much Promise' (1939) *Boxoffice*, 11 November, p. 24.

Inglis, I. (2012) 'Music into Movies: The Film of the Song', in D. Cartmell (ed) *A Companion to Literature, Film and Adaptation*, Oxford: Wiley and Sons, pp. 312–29.

Inglis, I. (2007) 'Popular Music History on Screen: The Pop/Rock Biopic', *Popular Music History*, Vol. 2, No. 1, pp. 77–93.

'It Was a Bumpy First Two Years, But Schwartz Sanguine Re DCA' (1957) *Variety*, 10 July, pp. 4, 24.

Izod, J. (1988) *Hollywood and the Box Office, 1895–1986*, New York, NY: Columbia University Press.

James, D.E. (2016) *Rock 'n' Film: Cinema's Dance with Popular Music*, New York, NY: Oxford University Press.

'Kahl & Levy Tie up Freed Movie Score' (1956) *Billboard*, 24 November, p. 15.

'Katzman Inks Columbia Serial Production Deal' (1945) *Hollywood Reporter*, 21 September, p. 3.

'Katzman Musical to Roll' (1955) *Hollywood Reporter*, 14 November, p. 4.

'Katzman Rolls "Mohican": First in New Col Pact' (1946) *Hollywood Reporter*, 21 June, p. 2.

Kindem, G.A. (1979) 'Hollywood's Conversion to Color: The Technological, Economic and Aesthetic Factors', *Journal of the University Film Association*, Vol. 31, No. 2, Spring, pp. 29–36.

Klein, A.A. (2011) *American Film Cycles: Reframing Genres, Screening Social Problems, and Defining Subcultures*, Austin, TX: University of Texas Press.

Kramer, G. (1956) '"Rock, Rock, Rock!" Jumbo Size Disk Talent Package', *Billboard*, 8 December, p. 22.

Leitch, T. (2009) 'Postliterary Adaptation', in T. Leitch, *Film Adaptation and Its Discontents: From Gone with the Wind to The Passion of the Christ*, Baltimore, MD: Johns Hopkins University Press, pp. 257–79.

Lev, P. (2013) *Twentieth Century-Fox: The Zanuck-Skouras Years, 1935–1965*, Austin, TX: University of Texas Press.

Lev, P. (2006) *The Fifties: Transforming the Screen 1950–1959*, Berkeley, CA: University of California Press.

'Low-Budget Combo a $110,000 Surprise' (1956) *Hollywood Reporter*, 11 September, pp. 3, 11.

Matza, D. (1962) 'Position and Behaviour Patterns of Youth', in E. Paris (ed) *Handbook of Modern Sociology*, New York, NY: Rand McNally, pp. 191–216.

Matthews, S. (1984) 'Evan Hunter's Success Came Out of the "Jungle"', *News Tribune*, online, 7 October, p. E-8, www.newspapers.com/clip/99062220/article-on-evan-hunter/.

McNelis, T. (2013) 'Dancing in the Nostalgia Factory: Anachronistic Music in *Dirty Dancing*', in Y. Tzioumakis and S. Lincoln (eds) *The Time of Our Lives: Dirty Dancing and Popular Culture*, Detroit, MI: Wayne State University Press, pp. 239–56.

Medovoi, L. (2005) *Rebels: Youth and the Cold War Origins of Identity*, Durham, NC: Duke University Press.

Moffitt, J. (1955) '"Running Wild": Good Racketeer Drama', *Hollywood Reporter*, 1 November, p. 3.

Monaghan, T. (2008) 'Rock around the Clock: The Record, the Film, and the Last Historic Dance Revolt', *Popular Music History*, Vol. 3, No. 2, pp. 123–48.

Morris, G. (1993) 'Beyond the Beach: Social & Formal Aspects of AIP's Beach Party Movies', *Journal of Popular Film and Television*, Vol. 21, No. 1, pp. 2–11.

Mundy, J. (1999) *Popular Music on Screen: From Hollywood Musical to Music Video*, Manchester: Manchester University Press.

'Myers Makes Deal on "Rock" Pic' (1956) *Billboard*, 7 January, p. 16.

'New "Rock" Explosion of Hot Youth; Branch Mgr. Discounts Morals TNT' (1956) *Variety*, 2 May, p. 1.

Nicholl, D. (1964) 'Rocker Haley Set for a Big Revival', *Disc*, 6 June, p. 11.

'Nick Ray Eastbound' (1954) *Hollywood Reporter*, 22 December, p. 2.

'1954 Senate Subcommittee Hearings into Juvenile Delinquency Transcripts' (n.d.) thecomicbooks.com, online, www.thecomicbooks.com/1954senatetra nscripts.html.

'Note Book' (1955) *Hollywood Reporter*, 28 January, p. 7.

Osgerby, B. (2003) 'Sleazy Riders: Exploitation, "Otherness" and Transgression in the 1960s Biker Movie', *Journal of Popular Film and Television*, Vol. 31, No. 3, Fall, pp. 98–108.

'Pandro Berman Back' (1955) *Hollywood Reporter*, 11 June, p. 2.

Peterson, T. (1956) *Magazines in the Twentieth Century*, Urbana, IL: University of Illinois Press.

Prince, S. (2002) *A New Pot of Gold: Hollywood Under the Electronic Rainbow, 1980–1989*, Berkeley, CA: University of California Press.

'"Rebel without a Cause" Adds Four, Rolls Today' (1955) *Hollywood Reporter*, 28 March, p. 3.

Reinsch, P.N. (2013) 'Music over Words and Sound over Image: "Rock Around the Clock" and the Centrality of Music in Post-Classical Film Narration', *Music and the Moving Image*, Vol. 6, No. 3, Fall, pp. 3–22.

'Republic Okays Old Films for Tele; Editing, Rescoring to Fit TV Needs' (1951) *Variety*, 13 June, p. 3.

'*Rock around the Clock* Pressbook' (1956) Los Angeles, CA: Columbia Pictures.

'Rock 'n Roll: A Frenzied Teen-age Music Craze Kicks up a Big Fuss' [*sic*] (1955) *Life*, 18 April, pp. 166–8.

'Rock 'n' Roll Riots Don't Scare Haley' (1956) *Melody Maker*, 15 September, pp. 1, 4.

Rose, Cynthia (1980) 'Teen Dreams', *The Movie*, No. 43, pp. 841–3.

Schatz, T. (1999) *Boom and Bust: American Cinema in the 1940s*, Berkeley, CA: University of California Press.

Schatz, T. (1996) *The Genius of the System: Hollywood Filmmaking in the Studio Era*, New York, NY: Metropolitan Books.

Scheuer, P.K. (1958) 'Shocker Pioneers Tell How to Make Monsters', *Los Angeles Times*, 21 September, p. E1.

Schickel, S. (1954) 'Hot Lick Crews Muscling out Big Bands in Many Territorial Spots', *Billboard*, 31 July, pp. 20, 48.

Schoenfeld, H. (1955) 'Music: R&B in Big Beat in Pop Music', *Variety*, 19 January, pp. 49, 54.

Scott, J. (1983) 'The Wild Ones', *American Film*, Vol. 4, No. 8, June, pp. 30–5, 64–5.

'Screen Gems Brochure an Issue' (1966) *Variety*, 9 February, p. 7.

'Self Help' (1954) *The Independent Film Journal*, Vol. 34, No. 4, p. 5.

'"Shake" Adds Musickers' (1956) *Hollywood Reporter*, 2 August, p. 3.

'"Shake, Rattle and Roll" [*sic*] Aiming for 10,000 Dates' (1956) *Hollywood Reporter*, 28 December, p. 2.

Shary, T. (2005) *Teen Movies: American Youth on Screen*, New York, NY: Wallflower Press.

Shumway, D.R. (1999) 'Rock 'n' Roll Sound Tracks and the Production of Nostalgia', *Cinema Journal*, Vol. 38, No. 2, pp. 36–51.

Solomon, A. (1988) *Twentieth Century-Fox: A Corporate and Financial History*, Lanham, MD: Scarecrow Press.

'Special Handling Set for "Blackboard Jungle"; Seek Right Ad Copy' (1955) *Variety*, 16 February, p. 7.

Staehling, R. (1975) 'From *Rock around the Clock* to *The Trip*: The Truth About Teen Movies', in T. McCarthy and C. Flynn (eds) *Kings of the Bs: Working within the Hollywood System*, New York, NY: E.P. Dutton and Co., pp. 220–51.

Stanfield, P. (2015) *The Cool and the Crazy: Pop Fifties Cinema*, New Brunswick, NJ: Rutgers University Press.

Taves, B. (1995) 'The B Film, Hollywood's Other Half', in T. Balio *Grand Design: Hollywood as a Modern Business Enterprise, 1930–1939*, Berkeley, CA: University of California Press, pp. 323–50.

'Teen-age Musical Pic' (1956) *Hollywood Reporter*, 22 June, p. 9.

'"Tennessee Waltz" Steps out as Most Phenomenal Copy Seller in 15 Years' (1951) *Variety*, 17 January, p. 42.

'The American Film Industry in the Early 1950s' (n.d.) encyclopedia.com, online, www.encyclopedia.com/arts/culture-magazines/american-film-industry-early-1950s.

'The Exhibitor Has His Say about Pictures' (1965) *Boxoffice*, 26 July, p. A4.

'The Exhibitor Has His Say about Pictures' (1962) *Boxoffice*, 2 July, p. B6.

'The Luckiest Generation' (1954) *Life*, 4 January, pp. 27–9.

Thompson, R. (1975) 'Sam Katzman: Jungle Sam, or, the Return of "Poetic Justice, I'd Say"', in T. McCarthy and C. Flynn (eds) *King of the Bs: Working within the Hollywood System*, New York, NY: E.P. Dutton and Co., pp. 71–8.

'$300,000 Picture's Gross Expectancy Same as $1-Mil Film-Katzman' (1957) *Variety*, 1 May, p. 17.

Tropiano, S. (2006) *Rebels & Chicks: A History of the Hollywood Teen Movie*, New York, NY: Backstage Books.

'Two Editors on "Shake"' (1956) *Hollywood Reporter*, 24 August, p. 6.

Tzioumakis, Y. (2017) *American Independent Cinema*, 2nd Edition, Edinburgh: Edinburgh University Press.

Whyte, W.F. (1943) *Street Corner Society: The Social Structure of an Italian Slum*, Chicago, IL: University of Chicago Press.

Index

A Streetcar Named Desire (1951) 23
Academy Awards 6, 23, 51
adult; cultures 91; institutions 3, 20, 21, 29, 96; interests 20; management of rock 'n' roll 16; perspectives on juvenile delinquency 28; perspectives on rock 'n' roll 12; society 21; viewpoints on teen cultures 68, 70; world 22
affluent society, the 19, 22
'Ain't that a Shame' (1955) 55, 73, 110
'Alice's Restaurant' (1967) 86
Allied Artists 49, 51
American cinema: being more inclusive through B and exploitation films 75; and the meaning of exploitation 1; and *RATC* 8; and the shift from B film to exploitation film 45; and the shift from youth to teenager 16; and significance of 'Rock around the Clock' 109; and the use of rock 'n' roll music in 1950s youth films 31; and widescreen technologies 4; *see also* Hollywood cinema
American/US film industry 6, 8, 45–50, 63, 66; and adoption of location shooting 25; and the B film 46; and changing conditions 44; and development of the teenpic 8; established companies/practitioners 9, 80, 81; and exploitation film sector 1, 48; and film adaptation 83, 84; margins of 9, 44, 46, 61; moves from B to exploitation film 8, 48–50; production budget average 2,

70, 80; structure 45, 46; in transition 17, 50, 60; *see also* Hollywood film industry
American Graffiti (1973) 105, 109–110
American International Pictures 6, 49, 63, 70–75, 76, 81; and *Shake, Rattle and Rock!* 70–75
American Releasing Corporation 49, 70
American Society of Composers, Authors and Publishers, the (ASCAP) 10, 82n5
Archer, John 57
Arkoff, Samuel Z. 70
Arlen, Harold 35
Armstrong, Louis 104
Aurora Productions 6

B film(s)/movie(s)/production(s): and American International Pictures 71; *Blackboard Jungle* as a 66; and Brian Taves's taxonomy of 9, 17, 64, 79; and Columbia 52; and the double bill 46; duration 3, 48; era 50; focusing on youth 23; and Fred F. Sears 3; and low-end independent companies 46; and major studios 2, 46, 47, 61; and Richard Brooks 65; and *RATC* actors' credits in 2, 57, *58*; and Sam Katzman 2, 17; transformed to television programming 47; and transition to exploitation films 17, 44, 45–50; and under-represented audiences 75
Bad Day at Black Rock (1955) 64
Baker, LaVern 77

Taylor & Francis
by Taylor & Francis Group

Printed in the United States
by Baker & Taylor Publisher Services